Women and Monasticism
in Medieval Europe

Documents of Practice Series

This series, published by Medieval Institute Publications at Western Michigan University in conjunction with TEAMS, is designed to offer a focused collection of primary-source materials in a classroom-friendly format. Though the topics illuminated by these booklets are generally familiar to teachers and students in various fields of medieval studies, the booklets allow readers to concentrate on a single topic or theme, either as the principal reading for a specific unit or topic within a course or as a running supplement to topics and readings being used through a semester. The topics have been chosen so they either can be seen as focal points of attention on their own, or can be used to offer an historical dimension to material used in courses on literature, women's studies, the history of medicine, religious studies, and other such areas—areas that draw a wide range of students who are being introduced to the use of primary materials and to inter-disciplinary and many-layered views of the structure of medieval society and culture.

General Editor of the Series

Joel T. Rosenthal, State University of New York–Stony Brook

Advisory Editorial Board

Charlotte Newman Goldy, Miami University of Ohio
William Chester Jordan, Princeton University
Ralph V. Turner, Florida State University

Women and Monasticism in Medieval Europe

Sisters and Patrons of the Cistercian Reform

Selected, Translated, and
with an Introduction by

Constance H. Berman

Published for TEAMS
(The Consortium for the Teaching of the Middle Ages)
by
Medieval Institute Publications

WESTERN MICHIGAN UNIVERSITY

Kalamazoo, Michigan 2002

Printed in the United States of America

P 6 5 4 3 2

Cover design by Linda K. Judy

ISBN 1-58044-036-3

Library of Congress Cataloging-in-Publication Data

Women and monasticism in medieval Europe : sisters and patrons
of the Cistercian Reform / selected, translated, and with an
introduction by Constance H. Berman.
      p. cm. -- (Documents of practice series)
    ISBN 1-58044-036-3 (pbk. : alk. paper)
   1. Monasticism and religious orders for women--Europe--
History--Middle Ages, 600-1500. 2. Monastic and religious life of
women--Europe--History--Middle Ages, 600-1500. I. Berman,
Constance H. II. Series.
   BX4200 .W66 2002   2002009167
   271'.97--dc21

Contents

Part II
More Problematic Examples

Part III
Statistical Sources

Part IV
Narrative and Normative Sources

List of Figures

Acknowledgments

*P*ermission has been granted to use the map that appears here as Figure 1 and will appear in a forthcoming article in *Cîteaux* by Erin Jordan. I would like to thank Bernadette Barrière, Caroline Bruzelius, Karen Christianson, Patrick Conyers, Andrea Gayoso, Lisa Harkey, Erin Jordan, Meg Lande, Erika Lindgren, Wendy Pfeffer, Joel Rosenthal, Nicole Thompson, and Beth Zamzow. I owe a debt of gratitude to the entire staff of the TEAMS operation for their patience, and to the many undergraduate students at the University of Iowa who have "sampled" some of the following documents. I would also like to thank the University of Iowa International Programs, Vice President for Research, and Obermann Center for Advanced Studies for support while this project was underway. Benjamin and David have been as patient with this as all the other things.

Introduction

Religious Women and Religious Reform
in the High Middle Ages,
with an Emphasis on Cistercian Nuns

omen played a role in the history of monasticism from its origins in early Christianity. Early medieval communities of nuns were often "double monasteries"— women's houses and an attached men's house—and they were frequently ruled by a powerful abbess who came from a noble or royal family. However, many of these communities were destroyed in Viking invasions of Europe during the ninth and tenth centuries. In England, with the "monastic reform" movement of the eleventh century, communities of nuns often were replaced by houses of monks. While double monasteries, in this particular and full sense, generally are seen as institutions of the early Middle Ages, any community of nuns must be a double monastery in some respects, being dependent on at least one male to be its priest—since no woman could administer the sacraments or lead all the services. After A.D. 1000 new experiments in reform monastic life again included monastic communities not segregated by sex. Many of these new foundations may have been family monasteries to which priests and their wives retired in the face of strictures against clerical marriage during the Gregorian reform of the eleventh century. As some forms of monasticism reached into the world and provided "social services," some of the new communities staffed the hospitals that began to undertake some of the activities formerly performed by wives of priests.

1

The history of monastic women's role in the great reform movements of the High Middle Ages is only beginning to be written. We now believe that women were much more efficient at managing their properties than once was thought, and that many houses of nuns were in fact not poor. There has been considerable change in our theoretical approaches to nuns' acquisition and management of property—the topics on which the documents of practice throw most light. But this is only the tip of the iceberg in terms of new thinking about religious women, the efficacy of their prayers, the favor which their houses were shown, and the strictness of their enclosure.

Religious women's history during the High Middle Ages has been neglected because it was assumed that during what was characterized by Marc Bloch as a Second Feudal Age there had been a decline in the numbers of cloistered religious women. Older scholarship and work on monastic records *seemed* to confirm this. Documents from male houses certainly predominate in the materials published over the last century by local history societies. However, this reflects editorial and social bias, not the reality of what has been preserved (or of the medieval situations). There are many more documents about women and women's houses than is apparent at first glance.

Charters preserved for monastic communities of women provide a good starting place for elucidating the medieval history of religious women. Charters are private documents that began to appear in the early Middle Ages; they record legal agreements including gifts, sales, arbitrated settlements, and agreements about property, mostly of land conveyances between religious communities or other ecclesiastics and their neighbors. Some record transactions made between two monastic communities, but more often they record interactions between such communities and their secular neighbors. They tend to result from a specific incident—when religious houses are founded, when a patron dies and leaves property to that community in expectation of prayers, or because of a dispute that both sides attempted to resolve. These types of documents survive in relatively large numbers for the Middle Ages because they were written on parchment, which in comparison to paper is virtually indestructible, and because they often were copied into parchment books of charters, called cartularies. Most were written in Latin rather than the emerging vernacular languages, but often there are vernacular intrusions. Because they incorporate legalese, often in shortened form, they sometimes are virtually impossible to understand, but the greatest barrier to their use is that they can be excessively boring. Large numbers of them must be read through to extract bits of interesting evidence. However, most were recorded for the internal needs of religious communities and so have relatively less self-interest in their rhetorical presentation than we might find if, for instance, there were more autobiographies or chronicles from the time. In fact, for much of what we can know about medieval religious women, they are all that we have. I have chosen a sample of the more interesting ones.

We have charters relating directly to women's houses: their founding, their subsequent endowment, their external relations, their governance. Charters that do not seem to talk of a nunnery, or have been produced for it, still may tell us much about women's houses. Indeed, the archives for men's houses often include references to houses of nuns—sometimes such references to nearby women's houses are the only evidence we have for short-lived communities of nuns. The archives for men's houses show that women could be important patrons of monks; thus women's activities can be found among the "men's sources," and much can be learned about women and monasticism even from the published materials on men's houses.

But it is important to realize that the omission of nuns from standard histories in the past is not just a story of unpublished archives or too much reliance on medieval chroniclers. We should not ignore the fact that there are deeper reasons for the relative neglect of women's houses and nuns in the tale of eleventh- and twelfth-century monastic life and reform. Nowhere is this more obvious than with regard to the Cistercians.

The most famous reform Order of the twelfth century was that of the monks of Cîteaux, who were called Cistercians. These reformers often are described as having originated in a group splitting off from an earlier reform community at Molesme, who left there to pursue lives in harsher, more austere circumstances. Those secessionists moved to the site of what would become a new monastery at Cîteaux, citing as their reason for departure the lack of rigor with which the reform monastic life was practiced at Molesme. This is probably a justification developed out of hindsight, for there had been frequent foundations of satellite priories from Molesme. Unlike Cîteaux, most of those priories did not break away from the mother-abbey.

The first thing that most people know about the Cistercians is that their leader in the mid-twelfth century was Bernard of Clairvaux (died 1153, canonized in 1174). But Cistercian historians usually tell us that it was *not* Bernard who founded the first house of their practice. He was instead an adult convert to the religious life, whose powerful intellect and charismatic preaching led to the expansion of a congregation of houses under the control of his own Clairvaux. Only later would other houses associated with Cîteaux gradually coalesce into a Cistercian Order. By the beginning of the thirteenth century the Cistercians would be held up as the model of a new phenomenon, the religious Order, an "umbrella group" of individual abbeys. These individual abbeys were granted certain exemptions from local episcopal rule in return for establishing a regularized practice and undertaking a certain amount of "self-policing" in the form of regular internal visitation, to replace visitation and dispute resolution by bishops. Cistercians were undoubtedly important in the twelfth century, but we are beginning to question the pious platitudes that usually have been presented to explain their contributions to the development of religious Orders. My own work has questioned those old stories about the Cistercians primarily because the traditional explanations allowed no room for the many communities of women who were Cistercian nuns.

Scholarship on the Cistercians has had trouble accommodating the role of women in this new order. This is ironic given that abbeys of Cistercian women may have constituted the largest group of new religious houses for women founded in the twelfth and thirteenth centuries. Cistercian historians, falling back on a narrow reading of the juridical situation of women within the Order, generally have denied or minimized the role of nuns. Nuns have been ignored from the beginning, for instance in the mainstream Cistercian historiography, which may be traced back at least to the *Exordium Magnum* written circa 1200 by Conrad, abbot of the Cistercian abbey of Eberbach and formerly a monk at Clairvaux. This has meant that many materials, such as those collected here, lay untouched in archives for many years, even after women's history became an acceptable sub-field of medieval history in the last third of the twentieth century. In France there is still much that remains to be discovered in archives that were brought together following the French Revolution, and this is true for houses of Cistercian women from other parts of medieval Europe as well. Less survives of the churches themselves, but there are ruins, such as those for the abbey of nuns at le Lys, near Melun, founded by Queen Blanche of Castile (see Figure 2, p. 14 below).

Cistercian historians and many secular scholars who relied on traditional narrative accounts either denied the existence of Cistercian nuns or described those women as less than full members of the religious Order created by the Cistercians. It is precisely by using the documents of practice, the charters featured here, that we can show that there were indeed Cistercian nuns, and that they were a strong and valuable presence both within the Cistercian Order and within European religious practice in the Middle Ages.

What makes the particular charters presented in this booklet so interesting is that they prove or demonstrate the existence of those Cistercian women. They bring to light the many communities of Cistercian women that previously had been virtually invisible, showing that Cistercian nuns must be counted among the many types of religious women who existed in the High Middle Ages. In limiting my purview to Cistercian women, then, I have provided an example that is a good litmus test for assessing women's spirituality, activity, independence, and agency within the monastic world. At the same time, these documents tell us much about the medieval relatives of Cistercian nuns, the brothers and sisters, mothers and fathers who were founders, donors, and patrons of the women's communities, who made demands on their abbesses, and who expected to share in the benefits of their prayers.

Modern historians of monasticism have cited the inability of cloistered women to manage property and to perform mass; they have seen these as explanations for alleged financial difficulties in houses of nuns as well as for their limited autonomy. We do know that bequests to women's religious communities—whether for foundation or for subsequent support—were often smaller than those to men's, and that the churches and buildings constructed for women's communities were often smaller. Even those built by a queen, Blanche of Castile, could be relatively modest, at least in the case of le Lys. Recent scholarly work has shown, however, that some nuns' houses were generously endowed, that nuns could be particularly able in the management of property, and that it was held by many in medieval society that the prayers of religious women were especially efficacious. As we see in documents for Rifreddo (nos. 7–12), or Maubuisson (nos. 25–26), houses for Cistercian women were established by the most powerful laywomen of the thirteenth century.

Some critics of the time, and the modern scholars who have followed their line of argument, have seen nuns as subservient to the male clerical hierarchy, whereas we now interpret this as a way for them to concentrate on their religious vows. We shall see that subservience to men by these religious women is far from apparent in most cases, given the restraints of medieval society; even if they had lay-brothers to take care of business outside the enclosure, nuns like those of Rifreddo (see nos. 7–12) certainly did not give up control over property. When religious women did give up control of their material resources to men, it was often because such women were seeking to lead more Christian lives by practicing corporate or collective abnegation, as well as personal poverty, as we see at Coyroux (nos. 37–49).

Although members of religious orders were only a tiny fraction of the population of medieval Europe (perhaps one half of one percent), those nuns and monks produced most of the surviving administrative documents for the period up to 1250. One of the misconceptions about the production of such records, however, is that they were hardly ever produced by nuns. In addition to copying liturgical books and the classics of monastic education and spirituality, however, we have evidence that women themselves dictated charters, copied cartularies, and organized their archives in ways to best exploit their economic resources.

This volume consists of documents that I have chosen to translate from among the many thousands—mostly in medieval Latin, but occasionally in old French—I have read as part of my research about medieval religious women. There are two basic types of administrative documents here. Besides the charters that I have already explained and the medieval charter-books or cartularies in which those charters survive, I include several extracts from rent and account rolls. These show religious women and their patrons intent upon managing resources well. Whereas the accounts presented to Queen Blanche of Castile by the overseer of construction at Maubuisson (no. 62) may be most interesting for the light they shed on materials used, their cost, and on the methods by which monies were accounted for at the time, the rent rolls for Port-Royal (no. 60) and Saint-Antoine (no. 61) are interesting for what they say about the nuns as acquisitive managers of property. The records for Port-Royal, in particular, reflect efforts to organize monies due (or owed) by date and by type of payment; materials found in charters have been extracted and rearranged so as to facilitate rent collection. The list of Saint-Antoine's Parisian properties reflects somewhat less manipulation of the materials; it is more map-like—with properties listed by street and with rents due at various terms mixed together. But the Saint-Antoine list reflects the enormous wealth held by the nuns of that abbey, whose charters show that they acquired property rights within holdings that once had belonged exclusively to king, to bishop, or to the great Benedictine monasteries, and that they lent cash to tenants to improve their holdings—in return for permanently increased rents (no. 14).

There were often early links among such Cistercian women's communities. Those between le Tart or las Huelgas and their congregations or filiations often are discussed, but Saint-Antoine too seems to have been the head of a mini-congregation. Not only were nuns from Saint-Antoine sent by Blanche of Castile to found her abbey at Maubuisson but also Blanche later sent nuns from Maubuisson to le Lys, so that le Lys became in some sense the "granddaughter" of Saint-Antoine. Similarly, in 1225 nuns from a group of women near Sens who had been nursing lepers at Viluis were settled at la Cour-Notre-Dame and tied to the customs of the Cistercians as practiced by the nuns of Saint-Antoine. There were probably links as well among houses founded and supported by the countesses who ruled between 1206 and 1280 in Flanders, Jeanne and Marguerite of Constantinople, whose patronage is mapped on Figure 1. There are hints in the records of the thirteenth-century General Chapter that such ties among women's houses may have allowed them to resist some of the regularization that the ruling abbots attempted to impose on the Order's houses of nuns (no. 66).

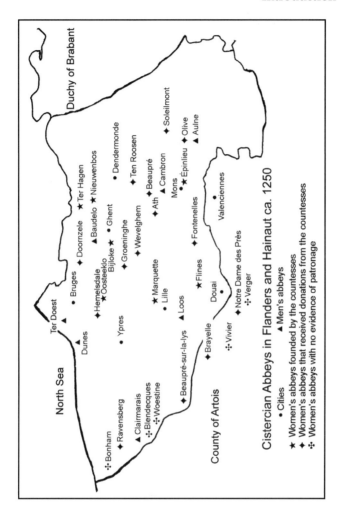

Figure 1. Map of Cistercian houses in Flanders and Hainaut supported by countesses of Flanders. By Erin Jordan, with permission.

The Cistercians were supposed to be one of the last rurally based religious Orders; this is how they always are presented in contrast to the urban reformers, like the Franciscans, of the thirteenth century. In fact, the situation is more complicated. Cistercians are well known for their managerial activities and economic success on granges in the countryside. But even in the twelfth century that success was tied to urban markets and changes in demand associated with the revitalization of cities in the twelfth century. Growing diversity in diet in western Europe in the twelfth century may have meant that demand for cereals flattened somewhat, but Cistercian entrepreneurs could overcome these marketing difficulties because of improved net yields. By regrouping fragmented agricultural holdings into granges on which lay-brothers produced surpluses, the new reformers still could sell excess grain profitably in nearby towns. Moreover, demand for meat and other animal products increased at the very moment when reform nuns and monks were tying pasture-rights together into efficient systems of transhumant pastoralism in which they optimized pasture use by taking animals to the mountain pastures in the spring and back down in the fall (such rights are mentioned in nos. 1 and 8, for instance).

By the thirteenth century it was clear that rural-based houses of monks and nuns such as those of the Cistercians also had to own urban properties from which to sell their produce; some eventually became Cistercian colleges. Thirteenth-century foundations for Cistercian women seem to have been located somewhat more in the proximity of cities than had been twelfth-century houses for either monks or nuns. Perhaps this is a result of the propensity of the Order to incorporate small hospitals located just outside the gates of major cities, some with lay-sisters and lay-brothers, many of them nursing lepers. Nowhere is this transformation of an independently founded hospital for men and women into a Cistercian abbey more striking than in the case of what became the abbey of nuns of Saint-Anthony-of-the-Fields, or Saint-Antoine-des-Champs-lez-Paris, just outside the eastern walls of Paris.

The documents offered below are typical of the vast numbers that can be found, still unpublished, in archives in Europe, or else published in various collections that I cite. To get to the heart of these sources one must wade through masses of formulaic, fairly standardized clauses to reach bits of information about the property holding and wealth of Cistercian women's houses. Many contracts do no more than confirm a pattern that only occasionally is made explicit in these documents. For an introduction to such materials, I have selected the more unusual, richer examples, which can cast light on communities and their patrons. In general, there is a glaring dearth of evidence on the actual everyday lives of religious women within the documents of practice, and few glimmers that illuminate their spirituality.

Reading charters for the evidence they provide regarding religious women—some of it direct and explicit, some indirect and muted—is an art or skill one learns in working with these materials. To facilitate comprehension in this introductory approach to what such documents can tell us and how they can be used, I have arranged the groups of documents to run from the least problematic and least difficult to the more obscure. This means starting with some thirteenth-century charters, since they are less ambiguous than those of the twelfth century. I have selected documents that give examples of the variety of communities of Cistercian nuns in terms of wealth or situation, or origins. Although most come from France, I have provided some indication of the widespread importance of Cistercian nuns by including documents from England, Italy, Germany, Spain, and even Cyprus. Charters are included for communities of women that were considered royal foundations, because they were made by Queen Blanche of Castile or her parents, but there are also documents for isolated rural houses of nuns that were originally hermitages. A few documents show how communities of Cistercian nuns often were closely tied to the medieval bourgeoisie in the thirteenth century. Of particular interest are the still unpublished records for the community of Saint-Antoine-des-Champs, which became one of the richest Parisian abbeys in the early modern period. Its surviving medieval documents show a community of Cistercian women increasingly supported by the patronage of wealthy Parisian citizens whose ambitions for their daughters had profound effects on the internal workings of the community.

Editorial conventions employed here are as follow: I have tried to include full documents, but in a few cases indicated in the head notes or by ellipses I have left out repetitive phrases or some of the excessive legalese that was creeping into documents by the thirteenth century. For clarity I sometimes have employed tense changes or rearranged the order of sentences. I try to indicate whether we are dealing with an original document or a cartulary copy and where placement in a cartulary provides additional evidence. I have identified kings and popes with their standard numbers and use Arabic numbers even though dates in the charters were written out in Latin words or roman numerals; I have done the same with the accounts. I give modern versions of dates whenever possible, but sometimes the day and month are not given. It is thus possible that a charter bearing the date 1101 was actually done early in the year 1102 because the day on which the New Year began varied from place to place in the Middle Ages (most often it fell in March, not January). Where days of the month are given in ancient and medieval forms, citing kalends, ides and nones, or saints' days, I have left them in that form in the charter text but have given the modern calendar date in the heading; see, for example, charter 5, in which the 3 nones of November (that is the third day before the ninth day before the ides) is, in fact, November 3.

I have translated the medieval Latin terms used for money into pounds, shillings, and pennies. The pounds and shillings in the charters were money of account with 12 pennies to the shilling, and 20 shillings to the pound, or 240 pennies per pound. Most pennies were by this time only about one-fourth pure silver. Although in the mid-thirteenth century, Louis IX began issuing a silver coin worth 12 pennies, the *gros tournois*, until circa 1250 only silver pennies were minted. By 1250 or so, all money circulating widely in France consisted of either the royal pennies of Paris or those of Tours; the royal pennies of Tours remained more valuable than those of Paris. Because most documents here refer to the coinage of Paris, only if some other mint is mentioned do I leave in reference to it. After the mid-thirteenth century Italian cities began to issue gold coinage for use in international trade, and France eventually did so as well, but the only gold coin mentioned here is an earlier Byzantine gold coin, the *byzant*, or *bezant*. The late thirteenth and early fourteenth centuries saw a rapid fall in the value of silver currencies; it was not a good time to be paid in money, as the nuns of le Lys realized (no. 31).

A few words require explanation. The word *monastery* was not used in a gendered way in the Middle Ages; a monastery could be a house of nuns. The Latin word *conventus* means community and is translated thus. Little distinction was made between *priory* and *abbey*, except that one had a prioress or prior and the other an abbess or abbot; there were priories of Cistercian nuns until at least the middle of the thirteenth century, as we see in the case of Moncey, discussed in note 36 below. Thereafter a regularizing trend within the Order led to the elevation of all priories of nuns into abbeys and their heads into abbesses. Often the charters use the nearly impossible-to-translate word *mansus*; I have allowed it to stand, but it originally meant a farmstead with lands sufficient to support a single peasant family. Similarly, the term *villa* in Latin still usually meant an estate, but it was beginning to mean a village. There are also a variety of terms for measures of volume, weight, and expanses of land that I have defined in a glossary at the end, which also includes various saints' days mentioned in the text.

The story told by these charters is that of how nuns and abbesses of Cistercian communities in the thirteenth century organized and kept records, managed their properties, responded to attempts at usurpation, and balanced their lives between the devotional practices that were so much a part of their cloistered world and the claims that continued to be made on them by family members outside the convent walls. The records available should help to reconstruct how women in the Middle Ages coped with wealth and with poverty—whether personal wealth and obligations (which they had inherited from parents), or familial property, which laywomen often managed for the lineages into which they had married.

Figure 2. Ruins of the church at le Lys. Photo by Constance H. Berman.

Part I

Charters for Houses
Clearly Those of Cistercian Nuns

Foundation Charters

*I*t makes sense to start with a selection of foundation charters for what are clearly Cistercian houses for women—thus those from the thirteenth century—because foundation charters often tell us more than other documents about founders and patrons and their motivations in creating religious houses for women. Although in almost all charters we can see the pious phrases that tend to be repeated from one to the next, or the amounts of wealth conveyed, such charters by founders often designate with great care the religious rule and customs, the heavenly patron to whom such a house was dedicated, and its relationship to other existing religious communities. Even what are commonplaces within the documents for a single house vary considerably over time. One interesting example is how houses dedicated to the Virgin Mary still refer to her in the twelfth century as Saint Mary but, by the thirteenth century, more often refer to her as the Blessed Mary.

I begin the selection of foundation charters with that for the most famous foundation for Cistercian nuns—one which soon was accepted, but treated as exceptional, by traditional historians. This is the abbey of las Huelgas in Burgos, Spain, founded by Alphonse VIII of Castile and his wife Eleanor (herself the daughter of Henry II, king of England, and the famous Eleanor of Aquitaine). This act might be considered the archetypical foundation charter for a Cistercian house of nuns. It is also important because one of the themes that runs through this collection of documents is how support for Cistercian women came from members of the family of Eleanor of Aquitaine, such as her Spanish granddaughter, Blanche of Castile, daughter of the couple just mentioned, who became queen of France and was mother of Louis IX.

The las Huelgas document was written in 1187, several years before the birth of Blanche. It shows her parents and elder sisters founding a house of Cistercian nuns that would become a favored place for that family thereafter; Blanche and her sisters must have visited often in their youth. Las Huelgas would be particularly famous for the power and authority of its abbesses, who were treated on a par with powerful bishops in Spain. Indeed, the independent activities by these rulers of religious women came to the attention of Pope Innocent III at the end of the twelfth century, at which time he issued a furious letter forbidding them from continuing to undertake "priestly" duties, viz., hearing confession and granting absolution for their nuns. The extensive power and wealth of the extremely aristocratic women of las Huelgas is clear in the grants made by the royal family when the abbey was founded. Among other rights, the nuns eventually would be granted rights to settle and tax any new Jewish communities in Castile. Their association with the royal house remained so close that the nuns habitually named a daughter of the royal family as their exalted female business agent or procuratrix, known as "The Lady" of las Huelgas.

A considerably shorter foundation document is that for the house of Cistercian nuns at l'Abbaye-aux-Bois (sometimes called Franche-Abbaye). This house of Cistercian nuns, located in the diocese of Noyon in the lordship of Nesle north of Paris, at a place called Beaulieu, was one of many houses for Cistercian women founded in the region between Paris and the counties of Flanders and Hainaut, where the countesses Jeanne and Marguerite of Constantinople ruled for the better part of the thirteenth century; their patronage of Cistercian nuns is mapped in Figure 1 (p. 9 above). We should not discount the relationship between the family of these two countesses and the founder of the Abbaye-aux-Bois, Lord John of Nesle, who acted as castellan of Bruges for the count of Flanders from this time until 1225. His foundation of a house for Cistercian women suggests mutual influences in favor of Cistercian women.

A third foundation document describes how the abbess of the house of Cistercian nuns at Saint-Mary-Magdalen in Acre decided to found a house of nuns at Nicosia in Cyprus. This charter shows how much the monks and nuns of the Crusader states had imported French religious practices with them to the East. Certainly, the same kinds of issues about who buried the dead, or who provided oil for altar lamps, came up in France. Of particular interest in this regard were, of course, anniversary masses for souls. No. 3 is a significant document in showing the authority and decisiveness of this abbess of Acre. Its careful discussion about who has authority over the new house in Cyprus, how an abbess should be elected, "by the saner, if not the senior, part of the community," may reflect the fact that lurking behind the scenes (but making no appearance in this document) is the person in charge of Cyprus at this moment, Alice, queen of Cyprus. Alice was another granddaughter of Eleanor of Aquitaine, who had much to do with establishing Latin practices in this part of the formerly Byzantine East.

More often the aristocratic ladies who supported Cistercian nunneries are the principals acting in the "foundation charters." We see this in Marham, as founded circa 1249 by Isabelle, countess of Arundel, widow of Hugh of Aubigny. Her status as an influential patroness is suggested by the reference to her mother, Maude, wife of William of Warren and daughter of William Marshall—regent for Henry III and the glorious knight made familiar to students of medieval history through the biography written by Georges Duby.[1] The list of witnesses, including several of her powerful brothers, confirms Isabelle's importance.

---

[1] Georges Duby, *William Marshall, The Flower of Chivalry*, trans. Richard Howard (New York, 1985).

Hers was an exceptional foundation in that she carefully secured documentation of its Cistercian status by first approaching a nearby house of Cistercian monks, then soliciting the General Chapter to send abbots to inspect the site. Thus armed with such documents, Marham upheld its Cistercian status against any efforts on the part of local clergy to deny either its part in the Cistercian Order or in that Order's exemption from tithes.

Next we have what may be considered a foundation document for the houses of Cistercian nuns at Lichtenthal in the diocese of Speyer. This charter was issued in November 1248, on the day of the consecration of "a new foundation of Cistercian nuns," by Ermengarde, countess or margravine of Baden. Her confirmation came several years after the first efforts to establish the abbey. We might ask, therefore, whether her confirmation at the date of the consecration of the church or that of the earliest documents should mark the foundation of this house of nuns, which still exists. Furthermore, we could ask if the fact that Ermengarde's document describes this as a house of holy nuns of the Cistercian Order is sufficient to confirm its existence as part of that international organization. Historians have suggested that a papal confirmation was needed in order to have a house of Cistercian nuns. In fact, such a letter was issued by Pope Innocent IV at Lyons in 1245 for the women at Lichtenthal, but Lichtenthal also was inspected in 1250 by abbots sent by the General Chapter at the request of Countess Ermengarde. Which was the defining characteristic?

Finally, in no. 6 we see an entire lineage of houses of nuns in the foundation of a new community at Saint-Sulpice near Albi by the abbess of Nonenque in the Rouergue, itself a daughter-house of the nuns of Bellecombe in the Auvergne. Nonenque was an abbey of Cistercian nuns that eventually was attached for visitation to the abbot of the neighboring abbey of Cistercian monks at Silvanès. Those monks began as early as the 1170s to claim that they had founded Nonenque, but there is reason to think that Nonenque had been there just as long as Silvanès. In the thirteenth century its nuns came to the attention of the Alamans, a family of officials who served both Raymond VII and Alphonse of Poitiers, counts of Toulouse. That family helped Nonenque in the foundation of a daughter-house of nuns at Saint-Sulpice, west of Albi. Many abbeys of Cistercian women were created in processes like the ones seen here. While these foundation charters appear to be unproblematic, in fact foundation charters are the very type of monastic document most likely to have questionable elements. Foundations almost always take place over a series of years, leading to confusing anachronisms as events are normalized into an account dated to a single year and day.[2] But the need to normalize foundation accounts for Cistercian nuns (and those of monks of the Order) reflects as well the fact that many were independent foundations, eremitical in origin, which coalesced into abbeys practicing Cistercian customs only gradually and whose origins must be reconstructed from documents such as those for Rifreddo (nos. 7–12 below) or Coyroux (nos. 37–49).

1. LAS HUELGAS, JUNE 1, 1187: Foundation by Alphonse of Castile and his wife Eleanor

In the name of the holy and undivided Trinity. Among all the other monasteries being built to the honor and glory of God, especially great merit is obtained from God by establishing monastic communities for women. Because of this, I, Alphonse, by grace of God, king of Castile and Toledo, and my wife, Queen Eleanor, with the consent of our daughters, Berengaria and Urraca, wishing for the remission of sins on earth and to obtain a place after this life with the saints in heaven, have constructed

---

[2] This has been discussed in a famous article by V. H. Galbraith, "Monastic Foundation Charters of the Eleventh and Twelfth Centuries," *Cambridge Historical Journal* 4 (1934), 205–22, 296–98.

to the honor of God and of his holy mother, the Virgin Mary, a monastery named Saint-Mary-the-Royal in the fertile valley or *vega* of Burgos where the way of life of the Cistercians ought to be perpetually observed. We give and concede this monastery for perpetual possession to you, Misol, present abbess of that community, and to all your sisters now and in the future to live there according to the way of life of the Cistercians. We also give to this monastery, to its abbess and its current and future community, to hold perpetually by hereditary right, and to possess irrevocably, all the inheritances, villas, lands, and possessions, cultivated or fallow, rents, fields, and buildings with all governance, and appurtenances as listed below.

These include all the agricultural inheritances and the rents that I, King Alphonse, own in the city of Burgos and in the entire plain of Burgos. Also my vineyards and a mill at Butheca, and additional rights over more vineyards, if the nuns want to plant them, and rights over the bathhouse of Burgos. I establish and command that no one be allowed to make another bathhouse in Burgos, and if new bathhouses are made anywhere in my kingdom, those establishments will belong to the nuns. In addition, I give to that monastery the enclosure of Arguisso and land along a stretch of water at Monio that extends from the bridge up to the old wine-press where they can freely build a mill, and I give watercourses and other buildings there according to the needs of the monastery. I also give the enclosed woodland at Estepar, and the inheritances I have in Bienvivre and Pampliga, where I give and command that whatever field labor the inhabitants of those villas have been accustomed to do for me should now be done for the nuns. I also give the rampart of Bienvivre, and the inheritance and taxes I have in Estepar, and the inheritance that Abbot Oniensis has in Saint-Felix, my inheritance at Quintanelle, my inheritance in Essar which was Garsie Ordonii's, my inheritance at Quintanella which is in Castrosoriz, my inheritance in the monastery of Rodella, my inheritance at Bervesca, at the wells or springs of Pinarus, and at the castle called Ordinales. Also, I give to those nuns a salt-works at Attencia that should produce a cartload of salt to be taken each day for the monastery; if those works do not produce sufficient salt, the deficiency should be made up from my other salt-works at Attencia.

I endow that monastery, grant it royal protection, and establish that anyone who presumes to attack it or its enclosure should be fined 6000 shillings. I transfer to that monastery all these inheritances and any income that once pertained to me from these inheritances. I establish that these possessions and any others which the monastery acquires from anyone now or up to the end of time, including those purchased by the abbess and the community, be treated as if they are part of the original monastic site, and be subject to the abbess and convent's power, lordship, and jurisdiction. Furthermore none of the payments, fines, or rights belonging to that monastery should be obstructed by anyone. All these rights should be free of any judgements, claims, or exactions from me, and should be absolutely exempt from all tax collectors, and shall remain so in the future.

In addition, I establish that whatever the nuns should sell, buy, or transfer for the work of their monastery, its conventual site and house, and its granges, will pay no tolls for cartage anywhere in my kingdom. Moreover, the animals belonging to that monastery and attached to its conventual site or its granges will have free pasture rights in all the woods and other places in which the king's animals have pasture. The nuns will pay no tax for their animals going up or coming down from the mountain pastures. Furthermore the nuns' shepherds' huts will all have the same protection as do those of the king. Furthermore, the nuns may cut wood, beams, and other building materials for the needs of construction of the monastery, its conventual buildings, and its granges in all the woods and places where those materials are cut for purposes of the king's construction.

All the above-written donations and constitutions will stand firm and stable for all time without violation. Indeed, may the full ire of the omnipotent God fall on anyone, whether coming from my own family or from any other family, who should presume in any way to infringe or diminish the contents of this charter. Indeed may he be sent off to suffer the inferno like Judas who betrayed the Lord, be fined 1,000 pounds of gold by the king, and be required to restore double the value of any damage done to that monastery. This act was done on the kalends of June, 1187. And I, King Alfonse, reigning in Castile and Toledo, commanded that this charter be made, and I sealed it, and confirmed it by my own hand. Gundissalvus, archbishop of the church of Toledo and primate of Spain confirmed this. . . .[3]

2. ABBAYE-AUX-BOIS, APRIL 1202: Foundation by John of Nesle and his wife Eustacia

In the name of the holy and individual Trinity, I, John, Lord of Nesle, currently castellan of Bruges, inform all readers of these words that I, being inspired by piety for the relief of the souls of the late beloved John my father and Elizabeth my mother, and for the relief of my own soul and that of my wife Eustacia, and for the souls of my brothers and sisters, and all my ancestors and successors, give and concede in perpetuity for the foundation of an abbey of holy nuns twenty bouviers of land in the measure of Nesle and the woods that are located above that land at a place

---

[3] *Documentacion del Monasterio de Las Huelgas de Burgos (1116–1230)*, vol. 1, ed. José Manuel Lizoain Garrido (Burgos, 1985), no. 11 (1187). There follows the seal of the king, those of his officials, and a list of confirming bishops in a first column, and a list of confirming nobles in the second one; then it says, "Master Mica, notary of the king, wrote this when Gautier Rodrigo was chancellor." The charter bears not the date 1187 but the Spanish-era date of 1225; at this time Spain still counted from the year in which it became a Roman province.

called in the vulgar tongue, Batiz. There those nuns can do what they want, including clearing the woods, if they wish. In addition, I have transferred to Eustacia my wife five muids of wheat in the measure of Nesle to be paid annually at my mill of Canteraine. This she has given of her own free will in perpetuity for the foundation of that house of nuns. I concede to those nuns my rights, lordship and whatever liberties I have in that land, saving only that I and my successors will be commemorated as patrons of that monastery. . . . So that this should remain firm I have caused this page to be fortified by the attachment of my seal. Done in the year of the Incarnation of the Word, 1202, in the month of April.[4]

3. NICOSIA, SAINT-MARY-MAGDALEN, 1222:
Nuns of Acre found a daughter-house on Cyprus

May all those who inspect these present words know that we, M., abbess, and the community of Saint-Mary-Magdalen of Acre, of the Cistercian Order, following the advice and admonition of our lord and reverend father, Archbishop Eustorgius of Nicosia, and with the counsel and will of the venerable father, Lord L., abbot of Belmont, with whom we are in unanimous accord, have decided that the house which we own on the island of Cyprus in Nicosia be given an abbess. Because no one already there is suitable to cope with the violence and other upsets, it has been proposed that a first abbess for Nicosia be elected in our house at Acre and be sent to rule in Cyprus.

Our entire community, or at least the greater or wiser portion of it, following God and the rule of the blessed Benedict and the observances of the Cistercian Order, should thus proceed to the

---

[4] *La Chartrier de l'Abbaye-aux-Bois (1202–1341), étude et édition*, ed. Brigitte Pipon, preface by Olivier Guyotjeannin (Paris, 1996), no. 1 (1202).

election of that abbess with our license and mandate. Either I, or whoever is abbess of the community at Acre at the time, ought to oversee this abbey according to the practices of our Order. If it turns out that no abbess of our house has been elected at Acre and therefore cannot oversee the election, the prioress or another discreet person at Acre will undertake oversight of election of an abbess at Nicosia. After an abbess for Nicosia is elected from among the community in Acre, she ought to go to our new daughter monastery in Nicosia and receive her benediction from the archbishop of Nicosia, making obedience to him following the practices of the Cistercian Order. This new abbess at Nicosia ought to have the same relationship to the lord archbishop of Nicosia that we have to our lord, the bishop of Acre, saving only the obedience which any daughter-house owes to its mother-house according to the practices of the Cistercian Order.

To promote peace, moreover, we wish that our house in Cyprus not be allowed to own any parish churches in Nicosia, nor, except by the license of the lord archbishop or chapter of Nicosia, should it receive anyone for burial. The nuns ought to receive oil for the lamps in their infirmary from the church of Nicosia in the same way that we get it from the church of Acre. Lest anyone question the validity of these arrangements, we, the venerable fathers, Lord Eustorgius, archbishop of Nicosia, and Lord L., abbot of Belmont, confirm this act by fortifying it with our seals.

Done in the year of the Incarnation of the Lord, 1222.[5]

---

[5] *The Cartulary of the Cathedral of Holy Wisdom of Nicosia*, ed. Nicholas Coureas and Christopher Schabel (Nicosia, 1997), no. 63 (1222).

4. MARHAM, 1249: Foundation by
Isabelle of Aubigny, countess of Arundel

Isabelle of Aubigny, countess of Arundel, extends greetings in the name of the eternal Lord to all the sons of the holy mother church who may see or hear these words. May all of you know that in my legal power as a widow, for the health of my soul and the soul of Maude, countess of Warren, my mother, and for the soul of Hugh of Aubigny, count of Arundel, my late husband, and for the souls of my ancestors and successors, I gave and conceded and with the present charter confirm to the abbess and convent of the Blessed Mary of Marham which is being founded as an abbey of the Cistercian Order in the manor of Marham, all my land there, with its appurtenances, which my father, William, the count of Warren, gave to me as my freely held marriage gift. I give this so that the said abbess and community and their successors will have and hold said land with all its appurtenances in free, pure, and perpetual alms. In doing this I desire that said abbess and nuns with their successors shall thus freely have and hold said land with all its appurtenances in lordship and homage, services, liberties, easements, and everything pertaining to it and in all things touching on that land in the same manner that I have or could have held it, freely and in full power. Thus I give it as freely and quietly as any alms are conveyed by any mortal. And I, Isabelle, and my heirs will guarantee and defend against all claimants in perpetuity the quiet possession of that land with each and every appurtenance by said abbess and community or their successors.

And in order that my donation and concession be confirmed and guaranteed in perpetuity, I have reinforced the words of this present charter with the impression of my seal. Witnesses to this are Lord Walter of Southfield, bishop of Norwich; Lord Richard of Wich, bishop of Chichester; Master Walter of London, archdeacon of Norfolk; Lord Roger Bigod, count of Norfolk and marshall of England, my brother; Lords Hugh Bigod and John of

Warren, my brothers; Master William of Sherwood, Lord Ralph of Hauteville. . . .[6]

5. LICHTENTHAL-IN-BADEN, 3 NOVEMBER 1248: Confirmation on its day of consecration

Ermengarde, countess or margravine of Baden, lets all those who see these words written below know . . . that for the remission of our sins and seeking the mercy of the omnipotent God, and in praise and honor of his glorious mother the Virgin Mary and all his saints, we have founded in the diocese of Speyer a new plantation of holy nuns called Lichtenthal-at-Baden in the Cistercian Order, and we confirm to it in perpetual possession the patronage over the churches in Ettlingen and Baden-Baden, the tithe at Iffezheim, the villae of Winden and of Beren with all their appurtenances, two hofs at Oos and one in Eberstein, and 12 talents of Strasbourg money from rents or cens at Selz which our sons Herman and Rudolf gave that abbey in pious devotion. In clear evidence of all these things and to make them endure perpetually, we have caused our seal to be placed on these words. Witnesses for these things are H., bishop of Strasbourg, and the abbots of Selz, Swarzach, Neuburg, Herrenalb, Bronnbach, the prior of Neuburg, the count of Wirtenberg; Otto, count of Eberstein; and many others, both clerics and laics. This was done in the year of the Lord, 1248, on the third nones of November, on the day of the consecration of the said monastery.[7]

---

[6] William Dugdale, *Monasticon Anglicanum*, ed. John Caley, et al., 6 vols. in 8 (London, 1817–30), vol. 5 (1846), 744 ff.

[7] Original parchment, photograph in *750 Jahre, Zisterzienserinnen-Abtei Lichtenthal; Faszination eines Klosters*, ed. Rosemarie Statmann-Döhler and Brigitte Herrbach-Schmidt (Sigmaringen, 1995), 192, description 193.

6. SAINT-SULPICE, 1267: **Nonenque founds a**
daughter-house between Albi and Toulouse

May all present and future readers note that in the year of the Incarnation of the Lord, 1267, on the first day of October, I, Agnes, by divine mercy, abbess of Nonenque, monastery of the Cistercian Order, in the diocese of Rodez, with the will and assent of the sisters: Clare, prioress; Aiceline of Auriac; Raymonda Cabrerie, sacristan; Willelma Rose, subprioress; Eliza, chantress; Marchise Lassine; Delphine Lombarde, pitancière; Borguine of Castro Marino, infirmarian; Jeanne of Creissols; Florence of Montalacri; Catharine of la Panosa; Saurie of la Tor; Blaise of Montclair; Eugenie of Belcapel; Margaret of Lampierre; and the other nuns of this monastery, give, confirm, and by this public instrument concede now and forever 150 shillings of Melgorian money to Esclarmunde Alaman, nun professed at our monastery of Nonenque, who will be prioress of the community dedicated to Saint Antoine and located at Saint-Sulpice, for the construction and enlargement of that community.

Similarly we release to that priory the entire honor that Sicard Alaman, knight of the castle of Saint-Sulpice, gave for the love of God to our monastery of Nonenque as inheritance for Aiceline Alaman when she became a nun here at Nonenque. The honor that he conveyed comprised the entire mansus and territory called de Vaissa Rabia with all its appurtenances located in the jurisdiction of Saint-Sulpice and adjoined on two sides by the honor belonging to Deodatus Cabonie, and on another by the public road which goes from Saint-Sulpice to the city of Vabres. This honor was given with all its jurisdictions, rights, appurtenances, access and egress, lands cultivated or fallow, grass, pasture, houses, woods, water, and whatever the donor had or ought to have had in that house and territory.

I, Agnes, abbess of Nonenque, concede all this property to you, Esclarmunde Alaman, lady prioress of the priory of Saint-

Antoine at Saint-Sulpice, who has received this transfer in the name of the community of nuns at Saint-Sulpice. Indeed, I give, cede, and concede it in perpetuity to you and to your community for your use and comfort by such a pact and under such conditions that by this contract Nonenque's abbess and its community will have in perpetuity the rights of patronage and visitation of this convent of Saint-Antoine at Saint-Sulpice.

I, Esclarmunde Alamand, prioress of the community of Saint-Antoine at Saint-Sulpice, humbly recognize having received this gift under the conditions set out, and that I hold this land by your gracious gift. I promise that everything will be undertaken as described. In devotion and humility I entreat God and the Blessed Mary his mother that my handling of this concession will merit our gaining the eternal prize. This was done in the chapter of the monastery of Nonenque, where witnesses were brother Gerald Manit; Raymond Gauscelin; Sicard, lay-brother of Silvanès; Bernard of Rupefort; Deodatus Vidal; William of Montalacri; William of Lunas; and I, Bernard Revelli, public notary of Versolz, who wrote this charter.[8]

---

[8] *Cartulaire et documents de l'abbaye de Nonenque*, ed. C. Couderc and J.-L. Rigal (Rodez, 1955), no. 88 (1267).

Reconstructing the Origins of Rifreddo

(O)ne of the first modern studies of medieval religious women to draw extensively on documents of practice was that on the house of Rifreddo in northern Italy, published by Catherine E. Boyd in 1943.[9] This abbey, located in the upper Po valley near Turin and not far from the modern border of France, was founded in about 1220 by Agnes of Saluzzo, daughter of Manfred II, marquis of Saluzzo. Agnes was the widow of Comita II, ruler of the Sardinian judgeship of Torres, and in one document she is called the queen of Sardinia. After the death of her husband in 1217, the childless Agnes returned to the Italian Piedmont to join her mother, Alice of Montferrat, countess of Saluzzo, who occupied a difficult political situation as regent for her underage grandson, Manfred of Montferrat, heir to the family holdings. Agnes purchased land from her nephew Manfred on which to build the monastery of Rifreddo, probably using the cash that had been returned to her from her dowry. There Agnes lived until her death in 1223. Her mother, Alice, who outlived Agnes, acted for the nuns in several contracts and is documented as entering Rifreddo before her death in 1233. The foundation of Rifreddo was confirmed in 1221 by Pope Honorius III with its community said to be following the Rule of Saint Benedict; it was to be directly answerable to the pope, to whom it owed each year a nominal tax.[10] But Rifreddo was soon Cistercian.

---

[9] See Catherine E. Boyd, *A Cistercian Nunnery in Mediaeval Italy. The Story of Rifreddo in Saluzzo, 1220–1300* (Cambridge, Mass., 1943). Rifreddo's documents were published in *Cartario della Abazia di Rifreddo [dalle origini all'a. 1300]*, ed. Silvio Pivano (Pinerolo, 1902).

[10] *Cartario di Rifreddo* no. 103 (1249) gives Innocent IV's interpretation.

Rifreddo's juridical situation changed as Cistercians gradually organized the visitation of houses of women within the Order. The abbey probably adopted Cistercian practices rather early, but retained its priory status, being elevated to abbey status only in 1249 (see no. 11). Particularly noteworthy is Rifreddo's incorporation of existing communities of religious women (nos. 8–10).

The charters show that Rifreddo's relationship with neighboring Staffarda was not happy. Staffarda's abbots came to covet some of Rifreddo's properties and tithe rights, and its abbot had to be reminded by the pope of his responsibility to provide the nuns with priests and lay-brothers (no. 12).

7. RIFREDDO, 14 MAY 1219: Purchase of villa of Rifreddo

In the year of the Incarnation of the Lord, 1219, seventh indiction, nineteenth day of the kalends of June in the presence of the witnesses listed, Lady Alice of Saluzzo, countess, wife of the late Lord Manfred, son of Boniface, marquis of Saluzzo, for herself and for her grandson Manfred, for whom she acts as guardian, sold and transferred to her daughter Agnes, who is the daughter of the late Lord Manfred, the villa of Rifreddo with all its honor, district, and appurtenances: that is, its rights to pasture, fishing, and hunting, cultivated and fallow fields, vineyards, meadows, and woods. Alice transferred all her rights, and those of Manfred, her ward. Henceforth Agnes or her appointees will possess Rifreddo as an allod to do whatever they wish there without contradiction from the aforesaid Alice or Manfred who together promise to be guarantors for this transfer or else to replace the transferred land with its equivalent or better.

In the name of Manfred and his heirs, and for herself, the countess Alice promised Agnes to uphold and observe the above. Alice promised Agnes that Manfred would confirm this sale by oath when he reached his majority at fourteen years of age. For all the above Alice obligated herself, all her goods, and all the goods of Manfred, renouncing any claims created by laws or Senatorial decrees for herself or him. This was done with the counsel and consent of Lord Guido of Polazaco, and in the presence and with the knowledge of Manfred, Alice's ward. Lady Alice, for herself and in the name of Manfred, accepted for this sale from Lady Agnes 500 pounds in the best coinage of Genoa, renouncing any exceptions for not having counted each coin. All this was done in the castle of Revello. The names of the witnesses were: Lord Gandolf, canon of Saviliano, Lord Alexius, judge, Lord Boniface of Polazaco, Lord Haymundus, who is called Papa de Veruca, Henry Bezamus of Saviliano, Milo Merla of Carmagnola, Otto Zussonus, and many others. I, Thomas, notary of the sacred palace, wrote this at their request.[11]

8. RIFREDDO, 9 JANUARY 1224: Countess Alice of Saluzzo purchases a monastic cell from the nuns of Caramagna

In the year of the Lord, 1224, indiction twelve, on Tuesday, the ninth day since the beginning of January. Lady Splendida, abbess of Caramagna, standing before Lord Jacob, bishop of Asti, swore over the holy gospels held by Otto Lawrence, that the monastery of Caramagna was weighed down with many usurious debts that could not be paid out of its funds. The bishop then gave permission to the said abbess to sell some of that monastery's assets and in particular to sell the cell of Saint-Hilary in the territory of Revello. Therefore in the presence of the bishop, and in the name of the monastery of Caramagna, the Lady Abbess Splendida sold for 300 pounds the cell of Saint-Hilary to Lady Alice, countess

---

[11] *Cartario di Rifreddo*, no. 6 (1219), confirmed in no. 10 (1220). Additional lands were purchased for 520 pounds by Agnes from her mother and nephew in the next year; *Cartario di Rifreddo*, no. 13 (1222).

of Saluzzo, who was acting on behalf of the monastery of Rifreddo. Renouncing the exception concerning not having counted every coin, Lady Splendida declared that she had received the 300 pounds in money from Countess Alice. She in return transferred to Alice all the immovable property of the church or cell of Saint-Hilary: that is, its fields, cultivated or fallow, grasses, pasture, meadows, vineyards, and woods in the territories of Revello and of Henuis, both in the mountains and in the plain. This included alpine pastures at a place called Calveto, as well as all rents, produce, claims, annuities, contracts, and debts. Whatever pertained to the church of Saint-Hilary was to be guaranteed to Rifreddo by the monastery of Caramagna for the value of up to double the price paid by Countess Alice. Then Countess Alice, acting for the corporate body of Rifreddo, promised that Rifreddo would pay to Caramagna one large *Byzant* [a Byzantine gold coin] on the feast of Saint Hilary each year for the buildings and lands of the church of Saint-Hilary.

This contract was done in the presence and with the consent of Lady Alice of Revello, Lady Sibilia of Quargento, Lady Sufia of Genoa, Lady Isabel of Turin, Lady Alda, the Genoese woman Jeanne, the Genoese woman Jacoba of Genoa, Alix of Lucerne, and Nicola of Braida, all nuns of that monastery of Caramagna, and Otto Lawrence, Tauronus, Peter Cocha, lay-brothers of that monastery. Lord Jacob, bishop of Asti, consented to and confirmed all this by the authority of the church of Asti. Done at Caramagna in that monastery. Witnesses gathered there were John, chaplain of that bishop, Lord Anselm of Auterisio, Henry Passandus, Lord Manfred of Lucerne, Lord Sigismund of Magliano, Lord Jacob of Platea, judge; Lord William of Vincis, Lord Obertus Vercius of Alba, Jacob, lawyer of Asti, Ogerius Colorius of Asti, Boniface of Genoa, and many others. I, Ogerius of Sinio, notary, being there, was requested to write this.[12]

---

[12] *Cartario di Rifreddo*, no. 25 (1224).

9. RIFREDDO, 10 OCTOBER 1249: Lady Ruffina enters

In the year of the Lord, 1249, indiction seven, on Sunday the tenth day in October, in the house of Bergundius Saccus, notary at Moncalieri, Lady Ruffina of Moncalieri, wife of the late Gardellus, because of her own religious conversion, gave herself and all her moveable and immoveable goods into the hands of Lady Otta of la Roche, prioress of Saint-Mary of Rifreddo, who received this gift as prioress of that monastery for the honor of God, the Holy Church, and for her successors there. This was done with the knowledge and in the presence of Lady Agnes of Paxillano, nun of Rifreddo. Of her possessions Ruffina kept only some small change to distribute as alms. The prioress, Lady Otta, with the knowledge of Lady Agnes, received Lady Ruffina to the common table of the nuns of that monastery and had this document written by wise counsellors. Witnesses to these events were Pratus Gellatus, William, husband of Elene Vianese, and Rubeus of Tegerono. I, Bergundius Saccus, notary, wrote the requested charter.[13]

10. RIFREDDO, 1250: Lady Alexia gives herself

In the year of the Lord, 1250, indiction eight, on Wednesday the second of March, at Moncalieri. Lady Alexia, nun of the church of the Holy-Mary-Magdalen of Moncalieri, and acting on behalf of that church, gave herself, her body, and her soul along with all her goods to God and the Blessed Mary of Rifreddo. She gave as well the church of the Holy-Mary-Magdalen of Moncalieri which is built next to the hill of Moncalieri, and all the possessions of that church, and its moveable and immoveable goods; that is, everything, wherever it is, which pertains to that church. This

---

[13] *Cartario di Rifreddo*, no. 105 (1249).

was given into the hands of Lady Tebalda, abbess of Rifreddo acting for that monastery. The abbess of Rifreddo then received Lady Alexia as a nun and sister of that monastery, promising to provide her the same food and drink that are given to other nuns of that monastery. Witnesses to this were brother Obertus of Asti and brother Manfred of Asti, who were both Franciscans, and Melanus Truna. I, Gaurrus, notary of the sacred palace, witnessed and wrote this.[14]

11. RIFREDDO, 1249: Innocent IV confirms privileges

Innocent bishop, servant of the servants of God, to our dear daughter in Christ the abbess of the monastery of Saint-Mary of Rifreddo and the sisters professing the regular life in perpetuity there at present and in the future. . . . We respond mercifully to your requests that the monastery of the Holy Mother of God and Virgin Mary of Rifreddo in the diocese of Turin be taken under the protection of the blessed apostle Peter and under our own protection. We confirm that privilege with the following provisions. First, that the *ordo monasticus* following God and the Rule of the blessed Benedict and the institutes of the Cistercian brothers as chosen by you be practiced perpetually in that monastery of nuns and be observed there inviolably according to the decree of the Fourth Lateran Council of 1215. In addition, whatever possessions and goods the monastery has at present or can acquire, justly and canonically in future, by pontifical concession, the largess of kings or princes, the gifts of the faithful or whatever means, are confirmed to you and your successors permanently. They are as follows: the place where the monastery is sited with its appurtenances, the church of Saint-Hilary with its appurtenances, the villas of Rifreddo and Gambasco with their appurtenances, all of

---

[14] *Cartario di Rifreddo*, no. 107 (1250).

which your monastery possessed before you adopted the institutes of the Cistercian brothers. We also confirm the more recent acquisitions of the grange and possessions at Racconigi, and the tithes you own in the Upper Po valley, as well as meadows, vineyards, lands, woodlands, usage, and pasture, both in woods and plain, in water, mills, roads, paths, and all other liberties and immunities. Finally, no one should presume to exact or extort any tithes from you for the noval lands that are cultivated under your own management, whether gardens or holdings in fields, or from your fish-raising and animal husbandry. . . .[15]

12. RIFREDDO, MAY 5, 1249: Staffarda is to provide lay-brothers to Rifreddo

Innocent bishop, servant of the servants of God, sends greetings and apostolic benedictions to my dear son the abbot of the monastery of Staffarda in the diocese of Turin. Let it be known that our dear in Christ daughters, the prioress and community of the monastery of Saint-Mary of Rifreddo in the Cistercian Order in the diocese of Turin have asked that you who provide them with a visitor also provide them with two suitable lay-brothers to undertake business for them that would otherwise involve them in inappropriate travel. Those nuns have forwarded this devout request to us and we in turn command you by apostolic authority to provide them with those lay-brothers. Done at Lyons, on the third nones of May, sixth year of our pontificate.[16]

---

[15] *Cartario di Rifreddo*, no. 104 (1249).

[16] *Cartario di Rifreddo*, no. 100 (1249).

The Urban Scene:
Cistercian Nuns at
Saint-Antoine-des-Champs near Paris

Saint-Antoine was probably a hermit's cell that became a house of Cistercian women as a consequence of the preaching of the famous late-twelfth-century reformer, Fulk of Neuilly. Circa 1198, repentant prostitutes and usurers created there a hospital of brothers and sisters that in 1208 was incorporated into the Cistercian Order as a house of nuns at the request of the bishop of Paris. Because it was one of the first Cistercian ventures near Paris, Saint-Antoine's abbesses soon were complaining about the tendency for lay-brothers and monks sent to the city on business by the men's communities to demand food and lodging from the nuns. The abbey was located close enough to the center of Paris to become a favorite place for university students to practice their sermons; today despite crowded streets and traffic signals, one can still walk in less than an hour from its site on the north-eastern outskirts of the medieval city to the cathedral of Notre-Dame.[17]

Saint-Antoine's recruits and support came from two distinct groups: certain families of knights who served the king as household officers, such as the Mauvoisin and Montfort families who were leaders in the 1209 Albigensian Crusade; and the wealthiest members of the Parisian bourgeoisie, often purveyors to the royal

---

[17] Constance H. Berman, "Cistercian Nuns and the Development of the Order: The Abbey of Saint-Antoine-des-Champs outside Paris," in *The Joy of Learning and the Love of God. Essays in Honor of Jean Leclercq, OSB*, ed. E. Rozanne Elder, 121–56 (Kalamazoo, Mich., 1995).

household, such as the family of bakers to the Lord King. Its nuns seem to have attracted very little patronage from the Capetians. Still, among the earliest surviving acts for Saint-Antoine is no. 13, a charter of confirmation made by the mother of King Philip, the queen dowager, Adele of Champagne, in which she confirmed the complicated arrangements for the division of tolls at Lieu-Saint-Sauve made by a knight's widow named Amicia who was becoming a nun at Saint-Antoine. Queen Adele here acts as an authority before whom an act is being registered, rather than as patroness.[18]

In a large city like Paris there were several possible authorities who could add the authenticity of a seal to a contract. In no. 14 three conveyances to the nuns of Saint-Antoine were written up in a single charter by an official of the provost of the city of Paris; one donor provides money for the nuns' fur cloaks, another shows an increase in annual rent, presumably in exchange for a "home-improvement loan." Similarly, no. 16 apparently was recorded before an official, in this case from the ecclesiastical curia of Paris, but that is only indicated in the final sealing clause; it shows a highly educated priest with the title Master of the University arranging for perpetual prayers by the nuns for his parents.

Most of what we find for Saint-Antoine in the archives in Paris are parchment charters recording grants made by individuals to the nuns and the copies of such documents preserved in the

---

[18] Eventually this job of authenticating acts was done by minor officials, either those of the king (in which case there is an increasing likelihood of the act being in French, not Latin) or of the bishop of Paris. This registering of acts before such an authority, who places her or his seal "in order to fortify" its authenticity, marks an important stage in people's thinking about contracts, one at which the charter is becoming dispositive—the written text itself constituting the agreement. Yet less than one century earlier, in many parts of France and elsewhere (as for example in nos. 38–42 below), the common practice was to list those who had heard the act as witnesses, who could later attest, if necessary, to a transaction done by public actions. Indeed, we still act out vestiges of the oral, face-to-face transaction when we "shake" on a deal.

parchment and paper charter-books or cartularies made by the community. There are two cartularies for the abbey. That from the early modern period (A.N.S*4386) concerns rural properties. That from the fourteenth century (A.N. LL1595) includes not only the rent-roll of Parisian properties (no. 61) but also conveyances of property in the city of Paris to the nuns. One thing that is interesting, but also frustrating, about this cartulary is that the nuns did *not* copy every charter concerning any specific property but, rather, selected one or two charters and, having copied them into the cartulary, remarked, "And there are nine other parchments concerning this same property kept in a sack. . . ."[19] We can only speculate on their principles of selection. As for their reasons for not copying everything, we can imagine their thoughts: "Parchment is dear, so is the price of a copyist and ink, and certainly our sisters should be praying, not copying charters."

This medieval cartulary also contains evidence about the nuns' receipt of private spending money; see no. 17, which records such a bequest to the abbess; elsewhere she settles such income on certain nuns within the community. This brings up an interesting problem about under what circumstances religious women had private income (whether substantial sums or pocket-money for incidental expenses) or could inherit property. Saint-Antoine was not the only place where entering women brought bequests from their families—for their personal use as well as for the community. This whole question of personal versus corporate wealth among medieval religious women requires further work.[20]

---

[19] The copyist does add locations for particular sacks of documents, giving a glimpse into their archives when he adds, "This sack is on the third shelf of the left cupboard in the right-hand gallery above the church"; Paris, A.N. LL1595: for example, fol. 8v, or fol. 11r.

[20] Yet monastic practice made a strict distinction between personal poverty and corporate property, and such grants of income to individual nuns seem contrary to such norms. That this was a problem elsewhere also is suggested by no. 65.

Charters usually were made when land was being transferred. As a consequence, cash gifts to the church might not result in a charter record. An exception is found in the extraordinary generosity of Blanche of Paciac, a bourgeois woman who gave large amounts of cash to the community of nuns of Saint-Antoine, both before she entered that house and at the time of her entrance. The lands purchased with her money were extensive, and in this case an act recalling what had been purchased with her money (no. 16) has the seal of the abbot of Cîteaux, along with that of the community of nuns. Records of such gifts as Blanche's, or that by Amicia, the widow of a knight (no. 13), suggest that older boundaries of social class were being transgressed among women within houses of Cistercian nuns like Saint-Antoine, just as they probably were as well in the royal court at the time.

By the fourteenth century, Saint-Antoine was among the richest houses in the Cistercian Order, owning numerous properties in Paris and its environs and even more granges than those listed in Blanche of Paciac's charter. Its abbess was *seigneur* of the Parisian *faubourg-Saint-Antoine* and owned extensive properties there. Its holdings seem to have developed later far beyond the more than three hundred houses and properties listed at mid-fourteenth century (in no. 61).

13. PARIS, SAINT-ANTOINE-DES-CHAMPS, 1205:
Confirmation sealed by Queen Adele

Adele, by the grace of God, queen of the Franks. We make known to all at present and in the future that Amicia, widow of the late Reginald of Savigniac, recognizes that she had given in perpetual alms to the church of Saint-Antoine-lez-Paris, where afterwards she took the religious habit [i.e., became a nun], rights over the passage tolls collected at Lieu-Saint-Sauve. The monks of les Vaux-de-Cernay already had 20 shillings in annual rent to be paid them from these tolls, and so did the Templars. Thomas

Pateaules had 60 shillings. All of these holders had received those rents from Amicia, who holds lordship over those tolls. She has now given the liberty and lordship over those passage tolls to the church of Saint-Antoine, and does so with the assent and will of her elder brother, the knight Jobert Briard, from whom she held the rights over those tolls. He confirmed and conceded her conveyance to Saint-Antoine before us [Queen Adele]. Similarly, Amicia's brother, Philip, confirmed and conceded this before us. And seeking to give the strongest fortification to this gift, we Adele, ourselves confirm it with our seal, in the year of the Incarnation of the Word, 1205.[21]

14. PARIS, SAINT-ANTOINE-DES-CHAMPS, 1261: Three gifts including money for fur cloaks

To all those inspecting these words, Stephen, official in charge of water for the provost of Paris, sends greetings. He makes known that John Fleming [or John the Fleming], citizen of Paris, came before him. Appearing sane, uncoerced, and of sound mind, said John gave, quit, and conceded in pure and perpetual alms in perpetuity to the abbess, nuns, and community of the church of Saint-Antoine-lez-Paris an annual rent of 4 pounds of Paris money which he held over the house of the late John of Montreuil in the tannery of Paris located in the censive of the Lord King. Similarly he, John Fleming, conceded an annual rent of 100 shillings over a market stall which belongs to the heirs of the late Peter of Chateaufort [and] which is situated in the meat market at the Grand Pont of Paris. He also gave an annual rent of 60 shillings over half the house which the late John Hamelin had in the holdings along the river-bank belonging to the late John le Cras; this is also located in the censive of the Lord King. Similarly

---

[21] Paris, A.N. H 3853 ff., parchment original copy dated 1205.

John Fleming gave an annual rent of 5 shillings over the house of the nuns of Villars in the censive of the Lord King, which rent once belonged to Deodatus. John promised that he would guarantee this for whatever use it was put to by the aforesaid abbess, nuns, and community according to the usages and customs of France. So that this should remain firm he obligated himself and all his moveable and immoveable goods. . . .

Let it be known that Petronilla, widow of the late John called Matthew, citizen of Paris, recognized that she gave and conceded in pure and perpetual alms to the abbess and community of Saint-Antoine-lez-Paris, annual rents worth 8 pounds so that the community could have fur for their cloaks. Also, she ordered that the nuns should receive an additional annual rent of 20 pounds of Paris money annual rent to be paid at the châtellet of the Grand Pont of Paris on the feast of All Saints. She promised in good faith that she would not go against this gift in any way herself or have anyone do so for her in the future.

Furthermore, let it be known that before us Stephen called Barber and his wife Maria recognized that they had given and conceded in pure and perpetual alms to the said abbess and community 100 shillings of Paris in annual rent to be taken and received annually over certain manses in Paris in the vicinity of the gardens of Monceau in the censive of the Lord King, promising in good faith that they will not act against this donation and concession for themselves or others in future. Note further that 6 shillings increased cens has been established over two holdings: the house of John the Glassmaker in the vicinity of Saint-Medard, which is next to the house of said abbess and community that had once belonged to the late Peter called le Ber; and a certain house that was once that of the late Bonardus of Vannes adjoining the house of the late Hugo called Cuillier, which now belongs to the abbess and community. That said 6 shillings increase in rent or cens was transferred in alms to said abbess and community. All these properties are sited in the censive of the Lord King. In testimony of all these things, I, Stephen, placed on these words the seal of the provost of Paris in the year of the Lord, 1261, month of December.[22]

15. PARIS, SAINT-ANTOINE-DES-CHAMPS, 1277: Sister Blanche of Paciac's gifts are recognized

To all those seeing these present words, greetings in the eternal Lord from Brother John, abbot of Cîteaux. We wish it to be known that we have been told by the nun, Sister Agnes, abbess of the monastery of Saint-Antoine-lez-Paris and the community there that Sister Blanche of Paciac, now nun of the monastery of Saint-Antoine, gave and conceded to Saint-Antoine and to its community annual rents worth 400 pounds of Paris money. After Blanche took the religious habit and entered Saint-Antoine she gave an additional 1,500 pounds of the money of Tours in cash, which was used by the monastery to purchase the following possessions:

The manor house located next to Champagnes at Belmont, which had belonged to Lord Thibault of Champagnes, with all its appurtenances. At the same place three arpents of arable land next to the strip of cultivated land belonging to the knight, Lord John of Champagnes. A quarter part in the produce from the common fields adjoining Saint-Antoine's grange at Savigny, and four arpents of arable land next to the *sauveté* of Saint-Antoine. In the territory of Praelles, four arpents of land and two arpents above the fishponds. At Montreuil, the Majorissoy winepress with its appurtenances. Eight pounds of annual rent over the passage tolls at Franqueville. An annual rent of 100 shillings over a house in Paris located across from the court of the Lord King in the censive of Saint-Magloire. At the grange of Bordes, fifteen arpents of arable land.

---

[22] Paris, A.N. LL1595, fols. 36v–37r (1261).

So that the gifts made by sister Blanche and the acquisitions made from her money be remembered perpetually at the monastery of Saint-Antoine after her death and so that she be commemorated in the prayers of those nuns serving God there, we have placed our seal, along with that of the nuns, on these present words, at the request of the abbess and community in the year of the Lord, 1277, in the month of November.[23]

16. PARIS, SAINT-ANTOINE-DES-CHAMPS, 1278:
Rent for anniversary mass

A controversy had arisen between Master Aimeric of Saint-Christophe, canon of Saint-John-the-Round of Paris and the abbess and community of the monastery of Saint-Antoine over an annual rent of 14 shillings that the nuns say they are owed over a house belonging to Master Aimeric located near their monastery and outside the walls of Paris near the Petit Pont. It adjoins on one side the house of Marie, wife of Reginald Barberii, and on the other the house of Anthony Triparii. An accord was reached, so that the nuns and their monastery should celebrate in their church annually on the Tuesday or Wednesday after the week of Easter an anniversary for the late Roger of Cherbourg and Isame his wife, the parents of Master Aimeric. The nuns should celebrate this anniversary just as it is customary and proper for such a mass to be said for one of the members of the community itself. If anyone else says he has any rights in these 14 shillings, Master Aimeric promises to give the nuns a different rent of the same amount payable annually over four terms. . . . In testimony of which Master Aimeric has had us place on these words the seal

---

[23] Paris, A.N. S*4386, fol. 75r–75v.

of the curia of Paris, in the year of the Lord, 1278, on the Wednesday after Easter.[24]

17. PARIS, SAINT-ANTOINE-DES-CHAMPS, ca. 1304: Private income of 10 pounds per year to abbess

May all those who see this now or in the future know that we, Margaret, lady of Beaumont, have, for the remedy and health of our soul and the soul of our late lord, the great in memory, John of Montfort, our greatly beloved husband, by our own hands transferred in perpetual alms for all time to the religious ladies, the abbess and community of Saint-Antoine-lez-Paris, a rent to be received from our land at Haties-sur-Orgue and its appurtenances, which include cultivable land, vineyards, meadows, and so on. . . . We give this rent so that our dear and beloved cousin, the abbess of said monastery, shall have these 10 pounds for her own use and wishes for her entire life, without any impediment from her community.[25]

---

[24] Paris, A.N. LL1595, fols. 5r–5v (1278).

[25] Paris, A.N. LL1595, fol. 73r.

A Foundation in Fulfillment
of a Crusader Vow: Port-Royal

*P*ort-Royal or Porrois was founded west of Paris, between Versailles and Chartres, in the area which is today the very fashionable suburban region of the Chevreuse valley. It was one of several houses for Cistercian nuns founded when important knights failed to fulfill vows to participate in the Fourth Crusade.[26] The foundation of Port-Royal began in 1204, when Matilda of Garlande received 15 pounds worth of rents to use for the soul of her husband Matthew, lord of Marly, a cadet member of the Montmorency family, who was about to depart on Crusade. Matthew died in 1205 before he had fulfilled his crusading vow, and his widow used the money to found a house of Cistercian nuns for his soul at Port-Royal.

Charters for Port-Royal are preserved in a two-volume medieval cartulary, the first volume of which had been completed by the mid-thirteenth century. At the time when the printed edition of this cartulary was prepared, historians such as de Dion, the editor of this cartulary, gave little attention to the internal ordering of charters within cartularies. In fact, de Dion placed the Port-Royal charters in chronological order in his edition and described the founder as the Crusader, Matthew of Montmorency. But historians have begun to realize that the placement of charters within cartularies reveals the motivations of the makers of those

---

[26] Another example was the Cistercian abbey for nuns at les Clairets, founded in the same year further to the west of Paris, near Nogent-le-Rotrou, by the countess of the Perche, Matilda of Brunswick—a granddaughter of King Henry II of England and Queen Eleanor of Aquitaine; *Abbaye Royale de Notre-Dame des Clairets: Histoire et cartulaire*, ed. de Souancé (Nogent-le-Rotrou, 1894).

charter books—telling us something about what people thought about their patrons and properties at the moment when the books were made.

Most cartularies open with charters from the primary founders—as we see below, for instance, in no. 35, the last will and testament of the founder of Lieu-Notre-Dame-de-Romorantin, which opens that abbey's cartulary. But the medieval cartulary for Port-Royal opens with a charter not from Matthew and Matilda but from their elder son, Bouchard, dated 1224 (no. 18). The 1204 charter in which Bouchard's father, Matthew of Montmorency, gave money for his soul is preserved, as is that dated 1206 in which the bishop of Paris explained how the foundation came about (no. 22 below), but they are the 58th and 59th charters in the medieval charter book. This suggests that by the time the cartulary's first volume was made, the nuns had come to treat Bouchard, rather than his father, Matthew, or his mother, Matilda, as the primary instigator of the foundation.[27]

The medieval cartulary opens with charters concerning a controversy over the tithes of Chagny and Escrone, which turned on whether lands cultivated by the nuns were tithe-exempt. The first charters reproduced here (nos. 18–20) make explicit the nuns' assertion that with regard to tithes they had the same exemptions as Cistercian men. The evidence for Port-Royal suggests that conveyance of tithes to nuns may have been considered a particularly efficacious way to endow communities of women. But it also served to solve a long-standing issue about Church property. Once the principle of a universal levy on medieval agriculture, in the form of tithes in support of the Church, had been established

[27] His mother is found in the second act of the medieval cartulary; see *Cartulaire de l'abbaye de Porrois au diocèse de Paris plus connue sous son nom mystique, Port-Royal*, ed. A. de Dion (Paris, 1903), no. 183 [no. 2 in the medieval cartulary] should be dated 1223/24, for Matilda of Garlande died on March 16, 1224 (see de Dion's charter no. 68).

in the Carolingian Age, tithes had fallen gradually under lay control. This became a concern of eleventh-century clerical reformers who saw lay ownership of ecclesiastical revenues as partaking of the sin of simony, more specifically, the buying and selling of Church office. In the twelfth and thirteenth centuries we see lay-owners returning tithes to the Church, often not by returning the tithes to bishops but by selling or mortgaging them to monastic communities—such as the nuns of Port-Royal—and thus getting the added benefit of monastic prayers. The issue becomes confused with that of papal exemptions from tithes granted to new religious groups such as the Cistercians.

Careful study of Port-Royal's charters suggests that the endowment and economic practices of its nuns varied little from what we have come to expect of Cistercian abbeys for monks. These documents also expand our understanding of the process of authentication of charters discussed above with regard to Saint-Antoine. No. 21, for instance, shows a conveyance made before the bishop of Chartres, who acts as the authority before whom donors have their conveyances recorded and sealed. Here the bishop also acts on his authority as bishop because he is confirming the transfer of tithes (which should have come to him) to the nuns of Port-Royal.

Most strikingly, these documents reveal a knightly class in crisis. Port-Royal's rent-roll (no. 60) shows local elites' support for this house of nuns. But charters that record multiple daughters entering the community here (nos. 23 and 24) and elsewhere (see no. 36, for Lieu) or that report sons of knights who are not being knighted (no. 36 perhaps) suggest a certain social upheaval. During the thirteenth century, not only did many women enter religious orders but also many men and women lost social class because their families had no money to have their sons knighted or to give as marriage portions to their daughters. Such requests for multiple daughters to be admitted to the religious communities that their families had founded a generation or two earlier contributed to the overcrowding found in many thirteenth-century communities of nuns, not only those of Cistercians. Concern arose among the clergy about limiting the size of nuns' houses (see no. 66); for Port-Royal in 1233 a limit of sixty was set.[28]

18. PORT-ROYAL, 1224: Bouchard of Marly gives land at Chagny

I, Bouchard, lord of Marly, make known to all who see these words, that with the assent and will of Mabillia, my wife, and of Thibault, my first born son, and my other sons, for the health of my soul, my father's and mother's souls, and the souls of my ancestors and friends, I gave and conceded in pure alms to the nuns of Port-Royal my land at Chagny, which I have held from Peter Gatteri of Escrones for a rent of 15 shillings paid by me annually at the feast of Saint Rémy. This land is located between the land of said Peter and that of Lord Hervé of Galardon, but is divided from their land by boundary stones. Each year on the feast of Saint Rémy the nuns will owe to said Peter the 15 shillings that I have been paying him. So that this should remain true and unbroken, I order that these words be reinforced with my seal. This act was done in the year of the Lord 1224, in the month of July.[29]

19. PORT-ROYAL, 1233: Annual rent ceded

May all those reading the present letters understand that I, Peter of Escrones, knight, gave and conceded to the holy nuns of Port-Royal an annual rent of 14 shillings in pure and perpetual alms. These are part of the 15 shillings annual rent the nuns owe me on

---

[28] *Cartulaire de Port-Royal*, no. 144 (1233) [*not* in medieval cartulary].

[29] *Cartulaire de Port-Royal*, no. 76 (1224) [vol. 1, no. 1 in medieval cartulary].

the feast of Saint Rémy for land which adjoins that of Lord Adam of Galardon and that of Lord Peter of Riqueville at Chagny. I do this with the assent of my wife Marie. Henceforth those holy nuns ought to pay me and my heirs 12 deniers [that is, 1 shilling, not 15 as before] annually on that feast as a nominal recognition for that land. With my heirs I warrant these alms to those holy nuns in perpetuity. In witness and support of these things, I cause these words to be fortified by my seal. Done in the year of the Incarnation of the Word, 1233, in the month of December.[30]

20. PORT-ROYAL, 1230: Tithe dispute resolved: nuns give up land in lieu of tithe

G. deacon of Chartres, and H. of Blois, archdeacon of Chartres, make known to all that Milo, priest of Escrones, made claims against the abbess and convent of Port-Royal asserting his church's rights to the ecclesiastical tithes on lands the nuns hold in the territory of Chagny. Those tithes, according to Milo, ought to be paid to him as part of his parochial rights, since the noval lands at Chagny are located within the boundaries of the parish of Escrones. The nuns replied that because they are Cistercians, they are exempt from any tithes collected on lands cultivated by their own hands or at their own expense. Moreover, the nuns stated that they themselves had brought those lands under cultivation at their own expense and therefore did not have to pay tithes to that priest. The priest replied that the abbess and convent had received those lands from the esteemed late noble man, Bouchard of Marly, and that even before transferring lordship to the nuns, the said Bouchard had already reduced to cultivation enough land to sow seven and a half measures of grain on it. The priest

---

[30] *Cartulaire de Port-Royal*, no. 145 (1233) 3 [vol. 1, no. 5 in medieval cartulary].

brought forward witnesses to show that he had rights to tithes on the lands that Bouchard had brought under cultivation. With the counsel of reliable men, an accord was reached and the abbess and convent transferred seven arpents of land to the priest and his successors, to be possessed perpetually by the Blessed Mary in the name of the church of Escrones. Because the nuns had for a long time cultivated the rest of those lands at their own expense, the priest gave up claims to those tithes. This peace having been approved by the reverend father, Lord G., bishop of Chartres, and by the venerable Stephen, archdeacon of Chartres, who was patron of the church of Escrones, this charter was made and sealed in June, 1230.[31]

21. PORT-ROYAL, 1228: Bishop of Chartres both registers and confirms tithe conveyance

Walter, by Divine Mercy humble minister of the church of Chartres, sends greetings in the Lord to all reading these words. You all should know that we concede and confirm to our dear in Christ daughters, the abbess and community of Port-Royal, the tithes which Simon, castellan of Nealpha, gave them which are for the parish of Saint-Rémy next to Alta Brueriam, and also the tithes which Simon of Logiis and Nicholas of Montreuil, knights, gave the nuns, which are in the parish of Montigniac next to the abbey of those nuns. In testimony of which we have ordered that the present words be made firm by having placed our seal on them in the year of Grace, 1228, month of July.[32]

---

[31] *Cartulaire de Port-Royal*, no. 121 (1230) [vol. 1, no. 12 in medieval cartulary].

[32] *Cartulaire de Port-Royal*, no. 191 (1228) [vol. 1, no. 45 in medieval cartulary].

22. PORT-ROYAL, 1206: Foundation confirmed by bishop of Paris

Eudes, by the grace of God, bishop of Paris, greetings in the Lord to all those inspecting these present words. We make it known that Lord Matthew of Marly once undertook to go to Jerusalem. He assigned 15 pounds of annual rents at Meulan for the relief of his soul, placing those rents at the disposition of me, the bishop, and of his wife, Matilda, so that we might confer and see to their expenditure and assignment. With the counsel of good men, we assigned and conveyed those rights to the church of Port-Royal in perpetuity. Later, after Matilda acquired the rent of a third of the revenues of the mill of Herchenout at Galardon, as well as half of the mill of Divisburg, and a quarter of the mill of Fréteval, she conceded in perpetual alms to Port-Royal ten muids of wheat of the best quality in the measure of Galardon in annual rent from the returns of those mills. But if, may God avert it, one of the mills should burn down, the nuns must be content with ten muids, of whatever quality. . . . Bouchard and Matthew, brothers and sons of Matthew and Matilda, confirmed and conceded the payment of this income to Port-Royal and so did Matthew of Montmorency in whose fief the 15 pounds of rents were located. In witness of these things which were done and with the consent of Matilda and her sons, I, Eudes, bishop of Paris, have affixed the impression of my seal to this charter in the year of the Lord, 1206.[33]

23. PORT-ROYAL, 1266: Two daughters enter

Greetings in the Lord to all those reading these words. I, John of Lagny, goldsmith, bourgeois of Paris, announce to all that with the will and consent of her community, sister Amicia, abbess of

---

[33] *Cartulaire de Port-Royal*, no. 4 (1206) [vol. 1, no. 59 in medieval cartulary].

Port-Royal, piously and without simony or any other sin, has received my daughters of minor age, Maria and Agnes, as nuns and sisters of that monastery. Knowing that God sees all things, and that if one makes a monastic house one's heir, it is impossible to die without heirs, I have made the following disposition of these daughters' portions. Not wishing to defraud my daughters in any way of their legitimate inheritance from me, I have conceded to Port-Royal a vineyard eight arpents in size. I also give to my daughters and to that monastery in their names 60 shillings of rents which amount to half of all my rights over a winepress called Press Comital or Conteignies located near Meudon. At the time of the vintage, the nuns will have the rights to have the fruit from four arpents of their vineyards crushed at that press by me or my heirs without any fee for usage or customs. . . .[34]

24. PORT-ROYAL, 3 NOVEMBER 1264: Four sisters enter

The officials of the châtellet in Paris extend greetings in the Lord to all reading these words. Let it be known that in our presence it was established that Dionysia, Sedilia, Agnes, and Margaret, daughters of the late Lord John (or Judas) of Coupières, a knight, wished to provide for the health of their own souls and bodies. Therefore, with the intention of assuming religious garb by taking vows of chastity at the church of the Blessed Mary of Port-Royal in the diocese of Paris, they have together made a perpetual gift between living people, purely, simply, and appropriately, and without any hope of revocation, to the abbess and community of that church and to the religious women of that monastery of Port-Royal. They have given themselves and all their mobile and immovable goods at Coupières and wherever else. They have ceded

---

[34] *Cartulaire de Port-Royal*, no. 306 (1266) [vol. 1, no. 41 in medieval cartulary].

them perpetually from this moment, transferring to the abbess, community, and monastery of Port-Royal all rights, lordship, property, possession, and whatever other real or personal claims, useful or direct, they might seek in those goods or which anyone might seek for them for any reason. These sisters, Dionysia, Sedilia, Agnes, and Margaret, promised without inhibition, comprehending clearly, and in good faith, standing before us in person, that they would not, for themselves or for anyone else, now or in the future, take any steps against the donation set out here, or revoke it for any reason. In witness of which, at the request of these four sisters, Dionysia, Sedilia, Agnes, and Margaret, we the officials of the châtellet of Paris, have caused our seal to be placed on this document in the year of the Lord, 1264, on the Monday after the feast of All Saints.[35]

---

[35] *Cartulaire de Port-Royal*, no. 303 (1264) [vol. 2, no. 51 in medieval cartulary].

Queen Blanche of Castile, and Her Cousin, Isabelle of Chartres

*I*n A.D. 1200 Blanche of Castile was brought to France by her grandmother, Eleanor of Aquitaine, to be married to the son of Philip Augustus, the future but short-reigned King Louis VIII (r. 1223–26). Blanche's uncle, John, king of England, paid her dowry, although probably it had been his elder brother, Richard the Lionhearted, who had arranged the treaty leading to the marriage. At the court in Paris the young Blanche would have encountered not only King Philip Augustus but also his mother, Adele of Champagne (no. 13), and between 1208 and 1212, Jeanne and Marguerite of Flanders, the granddaughters of Marie of Champagne, Eleanor and Louis VII's daughter. (The family of their other daughter, Alix de Blois, figures here as well, for Alix was mother of Isabelle of Chartres.) After Louis VIII's death, as regent for the young Louis IX, Blanche diverted funds in order to build a Cistercian house of monks at Royaumont, which would become the burial place for several family members as well as the place of prayer for Louis VIII's soul. By the time Louis IX came of age, Blanche had begun to construct an abbey of Cistercian nuns near Pontoise, Notre-Dame-la-Royale or Maubuisson (nos. 25–26, and no. 62). Blanche would retire there just before her death, and there she would be buried. It was normal at the time to separate internal organs for burial at other places, and Blanche left her heart to her second foundation of Cistercian nuns, a daughter-house of Maubuisson at le Lys near Melun (see nos. 27–31), to which it was duly transferred.

We have become accustomed to think of Blanche as the great instigator of Cistercian foundations for women in France, and Blanche's lifetime spent primarily in France coincides with a period of enormous expansion of opportunities for women within the Cistercian Order. Not only did patrons seem to favor them but also even the Cistercian General Chapter appears to have hesitantly turned its attention to the needs of Cistercian women— although such attention led to regimentation and regularization that the nuns resisted (see no. 66 below). But is there a causal relationship here or not? Other important women were also supporters of Cistercian nuns. We can see the support for Cistercian women in Flanders by Jeanne and Marguerite of Flanders in the map in Figure 1. And Blanche also may have been encouraged in her support of Cistercian women by Alix of France's daughter, Isabelle, countess of Chartres, who had inherited that county in 1218 following a failure of male heirs. While Blanche founded a house for Cistercian monks and two for Cistercian nuns, it is likely that Isabelle founded three houses for nuns, all pre-dating Blanche's foundations. The first was a priory of Cistercian nuns at Moncey on the Loire River near Tours. Very few documents survive for this house, whose foundation usually is attributed to Isabelle's first husband, Sulpice of Amboise in 1209, but Isabelle appears with him in the one extant charter recording his support, and after his death she makes a large gift for prayers to be said there for his soul.[36] In the 1220s, after the death of Sulpice, her

---

[36] See Tours, A.D. Indres-et-Loire, H799 and H800, where a medieval copy witnesses Sulpice, lord of Amboise, in 1214 granting rights at Ile Barbe to the nuns of Moncey with the assent of his wife Isabelle (here called Elisabeth, as elsewhere), and his son Hugh, daughter Matilda, and brothers John and William, and sisters A. and Dionysia. Another gift was made soon after Sulpice's death by Isabelle, for we have a copy of a confirmation of it after her death (therefore in 1249, although the document seems to read 1239) by Richard, viscount of Belmont, and Matilda his wife. This document records the gift of twenty-four sestiers, to be paid annually in grain and two muids of wine annually from the tithes of Amboise at the feast of Saint Rémy, along with 7 pounds of the money of Tours paid on the feast of the nativity of the blessed John the Baptist, to endow a priest at the church of Moncey to say daily mass for the soul of the late Sulpice. It must have been made between 1214 and 1218, before Isabelle became

inheritance of the county of Chartres, and her marriage to John of Oisy, Isabelle founded two more houses for Cistercian women: the abbey of Cistercian nuns at Lieu-Notre-Dame-lez-Romorantin in 1222 (nos. 35–36); and that at Eau-lez-Chartres in 1226 (nos. 32–34). Isabelle's final bequests for Lieu-Notre-Dame (in her will; see no. 35) suggest a close relationship to her cousin the queen.

Blanche's foundations at Maubuisson and le Lys were both strong communities that held extensive lands and rents; the enormous amounts that Blanche invested in Maubuisson can be seen in the account book for that construction, excerpts of which are found in no. 62. But when Blanche turned her attention to establishing a second abbey at le Lys, her son Louis IX may have concluded that she was spending too much on "her nuns" (see nos. 27–30). By then King Louis was focusing all the resources of the kingdom on his first crusade (1248–54), undertaken in fulfillment of a vow made when he had fallen ill and nearly died, and conflict over Blanche's lavish patronage of religious communities may have erupted in summer 1248 as the king departed on crusade.[37]

Le Lys was built for a considerably smaller community of nuns than Maubuisson, for about 10 nuns in comparison to Maubuisson's 120. It was endowed with payments in grain and money rents on the royal mills and granaries (nos. 27–31). Maubuisson, in contrast, had received great granges carved out

---

countess of Chartres or at least after her son Hugh died and she remarried. In 1288, Jeanne, countess of Alençon and of Blois (and Chartres reunited), and lady of Avesnes, gave the prioress of Moncey described as in the Order of Citeaux, in the diocese of Tours, two hundred three-horse wagon-loads of firewood annually; see also no. 66, item 64 (1243) below, where Moncey is discussed.

[37] Compare Philip Augustus's limits on religious bequests made by the wealthy heiress Eleanor of Vermandois, discussed by Louis Duval-Arnould, "Les Aumônes d'Aliénor, dernière Comtesse de Vermandois et Dame de Valois," *Revue Mabillon* 60 (1984), 395–463.

of the royal estates to the north and west of Paris, or purchased for the nuns (e.g., no. 26). Le Lys suffered from receiving income in payments from royal agents rather than having land under its own control, but as no. 31 shows, its abbesses vigorously resisted the efforts of those officials to commute payments of grain into money rents. Cost-cutting is seen even in the construction of the beautiful church, now in ruins. Unlike the churches built in the latest Gothic style for the nuns of Saint-Antoine and Maubuisson, both of which had elaborate radiating chapels surrounding their choirs in the east end, le Lys is a more restrained version of the fashionable Gothic architecture, with only two stories, and a simple flat east end with three equally tall lancets surmounted by a triplet of small roses or oculi; see Figure 2. Still, its ruins indicate the church's great elegance, if restrained in comparison to what was built at Maubuisson, Saint-Antoine, or some of the houses founded or supported by the countesses Jeanne and Marguerite of Flanders whose patronage of houses like Flines and Marquette was noteworthy; see Figure 1.

25. MAUBUISSON, 1241: Foundation by Queen Blanche of Castile of a house for Cistercian women at Notre-Dame-la-Royale, familiarly called Maubuisson

In the name of the holy and individual Trinity, Amen. Greetings in the name of the always eternal Lord to all those living in the Catholic faith who encounter these words from Blanche, by the grace of God, queen of the Franks. The doctors of the most holy mother Church have asserted that the blessed angelic spirits dance with joy when anyone is reborn at the baptismal font, but this is difficult to do in the present age except by going very far away to find someone not already baptized. Moreover, even if individuals have personally followed the life of the apostles, no human beings on earth may be assured of eternal life except by also acquiring the aid of celestial friends to plead their cases in heaven. Therefore with the assent of our dearest son, Louis IX, by the grace of God most illustrious king of the Franks, we seek the intervention of the saints who live already in their heavenly mansions, and especially that of the most glorious, always virgin, Mother of God, and of all the eternal city. Thus, for the health of our soul, and the souls of the late Alphonse, illustrious and well-renowned king of Castile, our father,[38] and Eleanor, queen, his wife, our mother, and for our dearest lord and beloved husband of great renown, Louis VIII, the late king of the Franks, and for our dear son Louis IX, and all our children, and all our ancestors, and our successors, we have founded, and caused to be created an abbey of nuns of the Cistercian Order which we are building and erecting in the diocese of Paris on the estate of Aulnay next to Pontoise. We shall call this abbey Notre-Dame-la-Royale because it is to be founded in honor of and in the name of the celestial queen.

In addition, we give and concede the following in perpetuity to the aforesaid abbey and to the persons to be placed there to serve God now and in the future: the place itself with the land on which it is sited, the monastery, the dormitory, the refectory, the cellar, and all the necessary buildings contained within its walls, with those buildings and walls themselves, and whatever is within them, from their length and breadth, to the right and left. All of which we have been acquiring with our own personal fortune, wishing and conceding that the abbess and nuns of that monastery receive all the aforesaid as pure, perpetual, and completely free alms, and that they possess them freely and quietly in perpetuity in order to live there the godly life of a community following most fully the rule and constitutions of the Cistercian Order. In order that the things contained on the present page be preserved in firm

---

[38] See no. 1 above.

perpetuity, we have reinforced them with the protection of our seal. Done in the year of Grace, 1241, in the month of March.[39]

26. MAUBUISSON, OCTOBER 1253: Sale to nuns

I, John of Villarius, knight, let all those inspecting these present words know that I have sold and give in perpetuity to the religious ladies, the abbess and community of the church of Notre-Dame-la-Royale next to Pontoise [Maubuisson], in the Cistercian Order in the diocese of Paris, three quarter-*arpents* of meadow, and half of five *perches* of vineyards, along with all my rights, lordship and justice. I sell this to the nuns for the sum of 8 pounds, 18 shillings which has been paid in full to me by those religious ladies and counted out in cash.

I hold the said meadow, which is located at Aulnay-Verneuil, from the illustrious lord, king of the Franks. That meadow is bounded on one side by the common pasture land of Aulnay, and on all others by those meadows which those religious ladies purchased from my brother, Econe of Villarius, knight. I give this to them and transfer to them justly, pacifically, freely, and quietly all hereditary rights, with rights to hold it in *mainmort*, so that the nuns may be possessed of those rights without contradiction, and without any claims being made of them by me or my heirs. I faithfully guarantee the part sold by me to the nuns against all claims. In testimony of which I have caused these present words to be sealed with my seal in the year of the Lord, 1253, in the month of October.[40]

---

[39] *Cartulaire de l'abbaye de Maubuisson (Notre-Dame-la-Royale)*, ed. A. Dutilleux and J. Depoin, vol. 1 (Pontoise, 1882), vol. 2 (Pontoise, 1890), no. 1 (1241, possibly 1242 n.s.); see variants in Pontoise: A.D. Val d'Oise 72H115.

[40] Pontoise, A.D. Val d'Oise, 72H141 (with a seal hanging from silk threads).

27. LE LYS, JUNE 1248: Louis IX confirms gifts

In the name of the holy and undivided Trinity, Amen. Louis, by the grace of God, king of the Franks, greets all those inspecting this charter. We wish to confirm gifts before we depart for the East, so that we may obtain divine aid for our endeavors and may also later taste the delights of paradise. So, for the honor of the omnipotent God, and his most glorious, and always Virgin Mother, we have founded and caused to be built using royal funds a monastery located next to Melun in the diocese of Sens for nuns of the Cistercian Order. We have named this monastery in honor of the blessed Mary for the health of our soul, and that of the pious Louis, once king of the Franks, our father, and that of our most dear, and illustrious Lady Mother Blanche, queen of France, and for all our ancestors in perpetuity. We have also given in perpetuity, and have conceded to that abbey and the persons serving God there now and in the future, the site of the monastery, dormitory, refectory, cellars, and each and every edifice within the ambit of the monastic walls, in their length and width, right and left.

It is our earnest desire that the abbess and nuns of that monastery should hold each thing we have conceded to them in pure and perpetual alms, with all freedom, so that everything the monastery possesses is held freely and quietly following the customs and the rule of the Cistercian Order. We give to the abbess and nuns serving God there, at present and in the future, twenty-five muids of grain in the measure of Sens to be taken from our granaries in Sens on the feast of All Saints each year in perpetuity. We also give 100 pounds in money from our provostry of Sens to be paid at Candlemas each year in perpetuity with a penalty of 5 shillings for every day after the due date that it is not paid. In addition we give to that abbey and its nuns fifty-four muids of oats in the measure of the Gâtine to be paid at the feast of All Saints. We also give in our forest of Byers two hundred arpents of woods in the place called Cauda de Pertus which have been laid out and marked for perpetual ownership for the nuns to do whatever they want with them. We also give from the dower rights at Melun and Corbeil of our dear lady and mother, the queen, with her assent and will, thirty muids of oats, ten muids of mixed grain, and five muids of wheat in the measure of Melun to be paid on the feast of All Saints each year in perpetuity, and 55 pounds to be paid by our provost of Melun at the feast of Candlemas each year in perpetuity, and 50 pounds by our provost of Corbeil paid on the same date under the same penalties. In order that perpetual stability be obtained for all these concessions we order by our authority as king that the present page be sealed with our seal. Done at Paris in the year of the Incarnation of the Lord, 1248, month of June, twenty-second year of our reign. . . .[41]

28. LE LYS, JUNE 1248: Louis IX's *Amortissement* asserting abbey built at his expense

In the name of the holy and individual Trinity, Amen. Salutations from Louis IX, by the grace of God, king of the Franks to all those seeing this page. We make known that we have founded a certain monastery near Melun in the place called le Lys with the intention that in it shall be a community of women of the Cistercian Order. That they may perpetually serve there for the health of our soul, the soul of our father, the late renowned Louis VIII, king of the Franks, as well as that of our illustrious mother, dearest Lady Blanche, queen of the Franks, and our ancestors, we transfer and confirm to the nuns of that place 20 pounds in annual rents paid by the provost of Melun which our dearest lady and mother, Blanche, has purchased from John of Sens, son of the

---

[41] Paris, B.N. Latin MS 13892, "Cartulaire du Lys," no. 1 (1248).

late Gervase of Sens. We also confirm 60 pounds annual rent paid by our provost of Paris which Blanche has purchased from our dear and faithful Peter of la Ferté and Eva his wife. We confirm the tithe and land at Syriac acquired by our mother, Queen Blanche, from the children of Brocenarius, knight, and his wife; similarly, the house, as well as properties at Chesutrias with the lands, meadows, and other appurtenances which our lady and mother, the queen, gave as alms to the aforesaid abbess and nuns, which she had purchased with her own funds from Lady Marguerite of Plessy and Odo Briart, the son of that lady, and from Ferricus of Aneto, John of Brics, knight, and the wives of those men. We concede to the nuns that whatever they have acquired up to this day from us or from our Lady Mother or from others in our fiefs or domains or censives, that is in lands, vineyards, meadows, woods, springs, pastures, houses, and other possessions by donation or sale or otherwise, should be held in mainmort and possessed in perpetuity. We also concede to that abbey and nuns perpetual rights to whatever they acquire in the future—whether by *inter vivos* gifts or in last testaments—up to the total value of 600 pounds of income annually. Such acquisitions are to be held in *mainmort* in perpetual possession, saving only that the nuns can never alienate those lands and excepting any cens, justice, and other rents owed to us for those properties. Moreover, in urban places the nuns should not acquire more than one house or two for their own use in any of our cities or castles.

Finally, let it be known that when we founded and endowed this abbey out of the goods of the king, and from our own hereditary property, it was our intention (as we establish firmly with the present privilege) that this abbey be under our protection and defense, and that of our entire realm. Moreover, the abbey and the territory in which it is sited will never be transferred to any other lord, but will remain with all its goods under our custody and protection, and that of all the kings of the Franks in the future. In order that this remain perpetually firm, we have fortified this charter with the authority of our seal, and as its words note herein, in the name of the king. Done in Paris, in the year of the Incarnation of the Lord, 1248, month of June, twenty-second year of our reign.[42]

29. LE LYS, JULY 1248: Louis IX grants woods and acknowledges Blanche's foundation

Louis by the grace of God, king of the Franks, makes known that we have conceded to the abbey of nuns which our dearest lady and mother, Blanche, illustrious queen of the Franks, established as a new foundation at le Lys near Melun in the Cistercian Order, free rights for now and the future to take wood and timbers in our forest of Byers, for constructing and repairing buildings within the enclosure of the abbey and at its two or three granges outside the abbey and its two mills. So that this present concession remain firm and stable in the future, we have reinforced the present words with our seal. Done at Lyons, in the year of the Lord, 1248, in the month of July.[43]

---

[42] Paris, B.N. Latin MS 13892, "Cartulaire du Lys," no. 2 (1248).

[43] Paris, B.N. Latin MS 13892, "Cartulaire du Lys," no. 4 (1248).

30. LE LYS, 1252: Blanche gives 300 pounds at Étampes

Blanche, by the grace of God, queen of the Franks, sends greetings to all reading the present words. We make known that our dearest son, the king, has taken the road to transmarine parts for the service of Jesus Christ. Before leaving he conceded to us the power to make additional gifts in alms for the remedy of our soul, those of our sons, and our ancestors, up to the value of 300 pounds in annual rents from the properties that we hold in dower. After the departure of our son, the king, we gave to the abbey of the Blessed Mary and the nuns serving God at le Lys near Melun of the Cistercian Order, which was founded by ourselves and our son, annual rents worth 100 pounds. We gave, in fact, 50 pounds in money to be paid every year by the provost in Étampes on the feast of All Saints, and fifteen muids of grain to be paid annually from our mill at Poignet near Melun.

Wishing to increase our concession of rents to that abbey of le Lys and the nuns serving God there, we now give and concede in pure and perpetual alms for our soul and the souls of our son, the king, and all our ancestors, an additional 50 pounds to be paid annually by the provost of Étampes on the feast of the Ascension. Furthermore, we wish and establish that the provost of Étampes make these two payments of 50 pounds at each term without delay, and for every day late, the nuns will be owed an additional 5 shillings. In witness of these things we have fortified this charter with our seal. This was done at the abbey of Notre-Dame-la-Royale near Pontoise [Maubuisson], in the year of the Lord, 1252, in the month of April.[44]

---

[44] Paris, B.N. Latin MS 13892, "Cartulaire du Lys," no. 10 (1252); an earlier gift from Blanche, no. 8 (1250), explains that rights at Étampes and in the mill at Poignet are part of her dower lands.

31. LE LYS, 1311: Payments in kind preferred to cash

Philip IV, by the grace of God, king of the Franks, makes known to present and future readers that our dear in Christ, the religious women, the abbess, and community of the Blessed Mary of le Lys near Melun in the Cistercian Order were given certain rents of wheat from our granary or mills of Melun or from our granary of Sens in concessions by the blessed Louis IX, once king of the Franks, our grandfather. These rents were to be received at certain dates each year and penalties owed if the nuns did not receive the rents on the due date. The nuns now complain that the rents in grain are not paid at the dates promised in the charters of the most blessed Louis. Instead, as the nuns have told us, those who administer our granaries and mills have tried to pay those rents to the nuns in money. Because of this and because of the inflated prices for grain lately, the nuns have suffered considerable loss. Having listened to their complaint and wishing to provide to those nuns the remedy they seek, we decree that the rents in grain which the most blessed Louis made to those nuns be correctly paid. We wish, concede, and establish that those holding the granaries and mills pay those religious women and their successors these rents perpetually at the established dates, and that the rents be paid in grain rather than in money or other equivalents under the penalties contained in the charter of the most blessed Louis IX. We command our current bailiff at Sens and any bailiff there in the future to assure that such rents be paid in grain on the dates due. The bailiff should make sure that those holding the granaries and mills do so and that any impediment to proper payment cease. That this agreement remain perpetually firm, we have caused our seal to be placed on the present words, saving all our other rights. Done in the abbey of Notre-Dame-la-Royale at Pontoise [Maubuisson], in the year of the Lord, 1311, month of May.[45]

---

[45] Paris, B.N. Latin MS 13892, "Cartulaire du Lys," no. 39 (1311).

32. EAU-LEZ-CHARTRES, 1229: Foundation by Isabelle, countess of Chartres, and her husband John

I, John, count of Chartres, and I, Isabelle, his wife, make known to all present and in the future that Nicholas, son of Guy, who was once major-domo for the abbey of Saint-Peter of Chartres, with the assent of the abbey and community of Saint-Peter of Chartres, conceded and quit-claimed to us for the construction of an abbey of nuns in the fief of Pantoisen, land and rights in the fief which he held as liege-man of the abbey of Saint-Peter of Chartres. These included two houses rented out by Nicholas (one the house of the late Raoul Huré with its appurtenances in the fief held by Raoul's children; the other that of the late Clement the Miller held by Eremburge, widow of Clement) which are in the fief of the heirs of said Nicholas. We have conceded and transferred whatever rights and justice the said Nicholas had in those houses and appurtenances, and whatever rights and justice are his, whether in tithes, lands, or anything else, to the nuns at Panthoisen [that is, Eau-lez-Chartres] as limited and ordained here. In exchange, commutation, and recompense for all the above, and for the rights and justice given to the nuns, we concede and give to Nicholas and his successors an annual rent of eight barrels of wine in barrels called *costerez*, which contain a sixth of a muid of Chartres. This was done in 1229, in the month of December.[46]

---

[46] *Cartulaire de l'Abbaye de Notre-Dame-de-L'Eau*, ed. Charles Métais (Chartres, 1904), no. 16 (1229).

33. EAU-LEZ-CHARTRES, 1235: Conveyance of rents to the nuns

I, William Meunier, knight, wish it to be known to all those who see these words that for the welfare of my soul and that of my wife and of my predecessors, I give and concede in pure and perpetual alms to the abbey of Eau in the Cistercian Order those 10 pounds in annual rent that the noble lady, Isabelle, countess of Chartres gave to me, which are paid annually at Easter from the tolls of Chartres. And the noble lord, John, count of Chartres, and Isabelle, countess, his wife, inspired by piety and at my request, provided their assent and confirmed this gift. In testimony of which things, I had this charter written, making it firm with my own seal. Done at Chartres, in the year of the Lord, 1235, in the month of October. . . .[47]

34. EAU-LEZ-CHARTRES, 1242: Conveyance of wine to the nuns

To all those seeing these letters, I, Isabelle, countess of Chartres, make known that when I founded the abbey of the Blessed Mary of Eau-lez-Chartres, I gave it three muids of wine at Valle Ferrici. I later gave another two muids of wine in exchange for the vineyards at Luisant which I had earlier conceded to them. Now again I give and concede to that abbey for the relief of my soul and those of my ancestors, seven additional muids of wine at my winepress at Valle Ferrici to be paid by my agent there. If there is any deficiency in those twelve muids of wine per annum, it is to be supplied by my press at Luisant. . . . This was done in the year of the Lord, 1242, in the month of October.[48]

---

[47] *Cartulaire de l'Eau*, no. 24 (1235).

[48] *Cartulaire de l'Eau*, no. 31 (1242).

35. LIEU-NOTRE-DAME-LEZ-ROMORANTIN, 1247: Last testament of Isabelle of Chartres

I, Isabelle, countess of Chartres, make known to all those who see these words that I, inspired by love of the divine and for the relief of my soul and those of my two late husbands, as well as those of my ancestors and successors, gave and conceded in pure and perpetual alms to the abbey of nuns at Lieu of the Cistercian Order, sited near Romorantin, which I myself founded in honor of the Blessed Virgin Mary and all the saints, all the lands those nuns held adjacent to that abbey as delineated by me. I have also given them two ponds next to that abbey which I have acquired for them for their free and quiet possession and ownership in perpetual peace, so that the nuns may use the water of those ponds according to their own needs, increasing or decreasing the size of those ponds as necessary. Furthermore, I give that abbey all my rents in kind at Morays, to do with it as they wish now and in the future, with all rights and lordship which I have there, which are estimated to be worth twelve muids of rye annually, and if those rents produce more than that, the excess should go to the nuns, but if in any year this property produces less than twelve muids of rye, the deficiency should be paid to those nuns on the feast of the blessed Michael by my foresters from the income of my forest rights at Brioud, with a late penalty of six sestiers of rye payable to those nuns for every day beyond the due date the rent is not paid.

I also gave to those nuns dues in the territory called Rapinae with all rights and lordship I had there, retaining only high justice for myself and my heirs. I gave and conceded to that abbey my rents on land at Mer and at le Pin, with all rights and lordship. I also desired and conceded that those nuns have and possess the rents over land with all rights and lordship at all the sites they have been given close to that abbey, either within the described territory, or elsewhere—excepting only the high justice which I retain for myself and my heirs. Also I gave to that abbey all my tithes from my vineyards at les Roullays, with all rights and lordship I have and possess there. I confirm to those nuns all rights in my woodlands adjoining the great pond belonging to them, but I will retain and keep all rights and lordship to an enclosed place that is separated from their woods by the road from Mer to the new mill and by the road from Romorantin to Corneil; it has been delineated by stakes. I also give those nuns all my woodlands at le Druillay next to the road from Millencay to Romorantin, except the one area that I have had enclosed there for myself, but this conveyance does not include usage beyond what I give explicitly. However, I and my successors will not allow those woods to become overgrown with brush for making them into hunting-grounds, nor will we otherwise decrease their value. In the woods that I have conceded to the nuns, I give them rights to preserve, sell, give, uproot, or reduce them to cultivation, and do whatever they wish in those places, both above and below the ground.

In my woods of Brioud and in all the woodlands of the castel-lancy of Romorantin I grant rights to collect fuel for the hearths within the walls of the nuns' enclosure, whether dead wood or branches, forbidding only the collection of fuel in the enclosed place mentioned. In my woods of Brioud and elsewhere I give rights to take green wood for construction and repairs within the enclosure of the abbey, again except in the enclosed place just described. I retain to myself and my heirs the high justice in those woods and all other aforesaid properties. To that abbey I have also given and conceded pasture rights to the nuns for all their animals in all my woodlands in the castellancy of Romorantin, whether covered with trees or not, saving only the enclosed place mentioned, where no cattle should be allowed to enter for the next seven years. I also have given and conceded the right to pasture as many as one hundred pigs in my woods and enclosed places.

I give to those nuns 60 pounds in annual rent payable on the feast of the blessed Hilary from the hearth-tax of Romorantin to be paid each year from that hearth-tax. Of this income, 50 pounds are to be used for purchasing wheat for making the community's bread. If those 60 pounds are not paid fully on that feast-day, the lords of Romorantin should pay 10 shillings for each day it is overdue. If the 60 pounds are not available from the hearth-tax, the difference ought to be paid from the passage tolls or oven fees of Romorantin. I also give those nuns another 60 pounds annually from my provost of Chartres payable by those who hold the provostry, half paid on the feast of the Assumption of the Blessed Virgin Mary, and the other half on the feast of the Purification of the Virgin. Again, if these amounts are not paid on those dates, 10 shillings penalty will be due for every day late. If there is insufficient income from the proceeds of the provostry, the then current lord of Chartres ought to make up the deficit from other rents at Chartres.

I also grant to those nuns the right to have a single burgher under service to that abbey in the city of Chartres who would otherwise have had to pay a personal tallage amounting to as much as 20 shillings. They can also have a burgher in my castle of Marchesner, one at Romorantin, and one at Millencay. These servants of the nuns are to be free and immune from all tallage, exactions, military or knight service, watch-service, witness duty, passage tolls, and all other customary exactions; when one dies or retires, the nuns may substitute someone else in each of these towns or castles, without any payment for this right.

For all the above conveyances, the nuns will establish in their abbey a chaplain who will celebrate the divine office every day, for the health of my soul and that of Lady Blanche, queen of the Franks, and for my husbands' souls, and those of my ancestors and successors. In order that these gifts and concessions remain perpetually firm, I have caused the present document to be forti-fied by my seal, wishing and ordering that the aforesaid dona-tions and concessions to these nuns be observed completely and without change in perpetuity by my heirs and successors. Done in the year of grace, 1247, in the month of May.[49]

---

[49] *Cartulaire de l'abbaye royale du Lieu-Notre-Dame-lez-Romorantin*, ed. Ernest Prat (Romorantin, 1892), no. 1 (1247) [opening charter in medieval cartulary].

36. LIEU-NOTRE-DAME-LEZ-ROMORANTIN, 1238:
Four of six sisters enter

I, John, count of Chartres and lord of Oisy, and Isabelle, countess of Chartres, my wife, make the following known to all inspecting the present letters. In our presence, Hervé of Tracy, squire, along with Agnes and Marlina, his sisters, affirmed and recognized that they had given their other four sisters in perpetual alms to the abbey of Lieu-Notre-Dame near Romorantin, so that those four sisters may be nuns serving God at that abbey. For the four sisters' inheritance portion from their father and mother, Hervé gave the nuns the new mills located on the Saldrina River in the parish of the Villehervé with all their appurtenances and customs. Those mills are given with the buildings sited next to them, with their land and possessions . . . , and with all rights to claim milling dues for those mills from anyone in Hervé's lands, rights to the fisheries associated with those mills, and rights to do as they wish with the islands that have formed below the mills. This is done saving only any earlier gifts in alms made from the revenues of those mills, and retaining to Hervé the woodlands and water-courses in the vicinity, although Hervé cannot change the water-courses which run to the mill-dam or otherwise divert water causing those mills to cease grinding. He will retain a small rent owed by those mills. And we, John and Isabelle, from whom the fief of these mills is held by Hervé, confirm and approve the transfer to the nuns of rights over those mills, saving for ourselves only the justice that we have over them. . . . Done in the year of the Lord, 1238, in the month of February.[50]

---

[50] *Cartulaire de Lieu*, no. 116 (1237).

Part II

More Problematic Examples

Coyroux/Obazine:
Double-House or Family Monastery?

$\mathcal{T}$his chapter and the next concern houses of nuns founded before the Order created by the Cistercians had really coalesced into what it would become in the thirteenth century. The evidence for both Coyroux and le Tart has been treated by traditional historians of the Order as anomalous and needing to be explained away. That for Jully has been seen as totally divorced from the history of Cistercian nuns. In fact, as I argue elsewhere, at these early dates, the Order had not yet become something to which some abbeys of monks or nuns could be seen to be attached.[51]

In the introduction to her 1989 edition of the medieval cartulary for Obazine, Bernadette Barrière described Coyroux and Obazine as part of what was a double monastery at Obazine founded at the beginning of the twelfth century by an eremitical reformer, Stephen of Obazine.[52] The community gradually evolved into two houses, that of Coyroux for nuns and Obazine for monks, and both eventually were affiliated with the Cistercians. Coyroux is often identified as the first house of women to be incorporated by what previously had been an all-male Cistercian Order, an event dated to 1147. But as no. 39 below shows, the site at Coyroux was not acquired until 1159 or 1160. Adoption of the practices of Cîteaux or affiliation to the abbey of

---

[51] See Constance H. Berman, *The Cistercian Evolution. The Invention of a Religious Order in Twelfth-Century Europe* (Philadelphia, 2000).

[52] *Cartulaire de l'abbaye cistercienne d'Obazine (XIIe–XIIIe siècle)*, ed. Bernadette Barrière (Clermont-Ferrand, 1989).

Cîteaux (not the same thing at this early date) was probably what necessitated the separation into two houses. In Barrière's view, the nuns sought to live humble, Christian lives, by ceding all control over communal assets to the monks. Her excavations have shown that the nuns lived at a more rugged site at Coyroux, in much less substantial buildings than the monks. They had a gatehouse with double portals, and a passageway between that acted as a medieval "air-lock." It allowed food to be delivered to the nuns without men and women ever seeing one another.[53]

Many women entered Coyroux and Obazine to become contemplative nuns, enclosed from the world and justifying their existence by praying for the community (as in nos. 44 and 45). But women also entered as part of family groups. No. 37 concerns devotees of both genders entering the community. No. 38 shows family members entering with rights to parish churches and tithes, which suggests that they may have been married priests with their families. Similarly, whether the female recluses or anchoresses noted in nos. 40 and 41 were wives or daughters of priests, it is likely that such women performed social service roles that earlier had been provided to local communities by priests' wives. In the context of the increased specificity of Church law with regard to the celibacy of priests, it is not surprising that we should find formerly married priests entering religious communities or their wives entering communities of nuns. But here the documents suggest that "conversions" to the religious life may have allowed married incumbents of parish churches to transform themselves, along with their families, into tiny religious communities. That this would have been a good option for clerical families "caught in the middle" of changing standards about clerical marriage may explain some of the expansion of new religious groups in the High Middle Ages.

---

[53] Bernadette Barrière, "The Cistercian Monastery of Coyroux in the Province of Limousin in Southern France," *Gesta* 31 (1992), 76–82.

The charters translated here are private acts, made by the community itself, in most cases. They are conserved in a cartulary rather than in the original, but even original charters from this early date would have been much less fully developed in their terms than, for instance, the foundation document for las Huelgas (no. 1 above). Many of these acts have only bracketed dates based on the names of bishops and abbots mentioned. I have included several series that trace the viscountess of Turenne and her family (nos. 46–49) and the Gourdon family (nos. 39–41).

37. COYROUX/OBAZINE, 1143–53:
Land and rents given when an entire family entered

This is the testament that Ademar Berengar made when he, his wife, and all their children relinquished the world and gave themselves for the religious life at the monastery of Obazine, giving all their possessions to that monastery, including their houses at Saint-Palladius, the gardens they hold there, a meadow, a vineyard, and a field at the mill-dam etc. . . . In addition, from the hereditary rights of his wife, Ademar Berengar gave:

Ten sestiers of rye as annual rent at Maranz, another ten at Longmont at Cessla, 20 pennies and a chicken there each year;

Lordship in the bordaria of Rotavulp;

The fourth share of the harvest from the mansus of la Genesta—Peter Austorgius acts as guarantor;

Two pennies over the garden of Gerald Rainald at Cérezac;

Two pennies over the house of John Bula;

The bordaria of la Faurga which is pledged for a mortgage of 30 shillings, etc. . . . [54]

---

[54] *Cartulaire d'Obazine*, no. 61 (1143–53).

38. COYROUX/OBAZINE, 1143–53:
Peter William and family enter as devotees

May those at present and in the future know that Peter William of Albussac and Almodis his wife, renouncing the world for a happier existence in the celestial fields, gave themselves and their sons as devotees to Obazine to serve God perpetually as paupers there.

They granted in perpetuity to God and the Blessed Mary into the hands of Stephen of Obazine, first abbot of that place, all their land and property at Albussac, that is:

Half of the lay-lordship of the church of Albussac;

Ten shillings rent from milling services in the priest's fief;

Eighteen pennies rent in milling dues, and services from Armand's house; Sixteen pennies rent for milling dues;

A quarter of the tithes, half of the wheat, and half of the oats in the fief of Boash and that of Bedenesch;

A rent paid in four sestiers of unthreshed wheat, and another four sestiers of threshed grain at Aimericos;

A rent of two sestiers from the cemetery garden;

Two shillings rent in the Condomina;

At Guioneschae 2 shillings, and 4 pennies, rent, etc.;

Two sestiers grain (one threshed) for the garden at Bucharet;

Three shillings rent for milling dues for the tithe of Bufeth;

Three chickens rent for the garden of Curtavret;

Rents owed for the house and garden of Peter the Jew: that is, 12 pennies on the feast of the Chains of Saint Peter, twelve on the feast of Saint Martin;

Four pennies paid from the proceeds of preparing cloth at the upper fulling mill, etc. . . .[55]

---

[55] *Cartulaire d'Obazine*, no. 103 (1150–59).

39. COYROUX/OBAZINE, 1159–60: Gift of the site of Coyroux

Magna, wife of Aimeric of Gourdon, gave the mansus of Coyroux to the abbey of Obazine. This gift was confirmed to Obazine by Raymond of les Genebrières and his wife Orbria. Listening were Peter of Puyblanc, John, cellerar, Stephen of Monceaux, and Stephen of Corneil.[56]

40. COYROUX/OBAZINE, 1152: Same family as guarantors

May those at present and in the future know that for the sake of his soul, Gerald Ugo of les Vaissières gave in alms to the monastery of Obazine the land and woods next to Penditz, as limited by boundaries already shown to the brothers of Obazine. Said Gerald Ugo and Raymond William also gave lordship there to Obazine. For as much of that property as was in excess of that given in alms, Stephen, abbot of Obazine, paid said Gerald Ugo 1,130 shillings of Cahors. Raymond William got 15 shillings. Arnold of Clairmont got 10 shillings. Aimeric of Gourdon and his son Pons got 80 shillings. Gerald Ugo confirmed his good faith by swearing over the four gospels. Raymond William confirmed, adding that neither they nor their descendants would ask anything more for this land, but they would always defend the abbey's rights. They gave as guarantors to Obazine: Bertrand of Gourdon, Aimeric of Gourdon, Pons of Gourdon, and Magna, wife of Aimeric of Gourdon. . . . This confirmation was done in the hands of Stephen, first abbot of Obazine, in the year of the Lord, 1152, seventh ides of November, luna six, when Louis VII was king of France and Gerald was bishop of Limoges.[57]

---

[56] *Cartulaire d'Obazine*, no. 195 (1159–60).

[57] *Cartulaire d'Obazine*, no. 534 (1152).

41. COYROUX/OBAZINE, 1168:
Sons confirm their parents' gifts

Aimeric of Gourdon, son of Aimeric, and his brother Pons, gave into the hands of Robert, abbot of the monastery of Obazine, confirming whatever their father Aimeric, or their mother Magna, or Pons himself, had earlier given to that monastery. This was done in the chapter of Obazine in the hearing of the community and of William of Belcastel on January 1, 1168, when Louis VII was king and Gerald was bishop of Limoges.[58]

42. COYROUX/OBAZINE, 1160–61: Gift of rights
over a house belonging to an anchoress

Armand Liapec gave to the monastery of Obazine all rights he had in the mansus of Albas Peiras, in the bordaria of la Cudeleira, in les Alys, whatever rights he has in the tithes at Obazine and at la Salesca, rights in the fields next to the Corrèze River, in the mansus of Furnols, and whatever rights he has in the holdings of the anchoress at Damnach. He gave all this into the hand of Gerald, second abbot of Obazine, in the hearing of John cellerar, Stephen of Corneil, Bernard of Saint-Ardei, Godfrey of Martemnach, Bertrand of Corneil, Evrard of Pauli, and William of les Ferrières. Done in the chapter of Obazine in the year of Incarnation of the Lord, 1160, when Louis VII was king, and Gerald was bishop of Limoges.[59]

---

[58] *Cartulaire d'Obazine*, no. 284 (1168).

[59] *Cartulaire d'Obazine*, no. 141 (1160–61).

43. COYROUX/OBAZINE, 1164:
Another gift concerning anchoresses at Damnach

Richarda, wife of Peter of Malfort, and their son Guy, gave to
Obazine whatever rights they held in the mansus of Furnols,
which Obazine owned, and in the tithes over that mansus, and in
a place called la Chambon de la Passière, as well as 8 pennies of
rent owed to those donors for land at Chaumont. The donors also
gave up claims at les Verrières and over the houses of the
anchoresses at Damnach. These gifts were made into the hands
of Robert, abbot of Obazine, in the hearing of John of Bordas,
Peter of Semur, Stephen of Monceaux, Bernard of Saint-Ardei,
Raoul of Arcas, and Ademar of Solac. Done in the year of the
Incarnation of the Lord, 1164, when Louis VII was king and
Gerald was bishop of Limoges.[60]

44. COYROUX/OBAZINE, 1168:
A gift made when a nun entered

Gerald Fulk of Turenne gave to Obazine all the rights he had in
the mansus of Velmespol, in that of Raigada, and in the bordaria
next to Baudran, for his daughter Plazensa, when she became a
nun of that house. This was done into the hands of abbot Robert
in the hearing of Peter, prior, Stephen of Monceaux, Bernard of
la Vaissière, priest, Ugo Faidit, and Gerald Pistor, in the year of
the Incarnation of the Lord, 1168, when Louis VII was king and
Gerald was bishop of Limoges.[61]

---

[60] *Cartulaire d'Obazine*, no. 194 (1164).

[61] *Cartulaire d'Obazine*, no. 280 (1168–69).

45. COYROUX/OBAZINE, 1170: Gift for a woman's entrance

Peter Arnold of Saint-Michel and William his brother gave a meadow located at les Banières to the abbey of Obazine. This was done when their mother became a nun at that monastery and in repayment of the 200 shillings which abbot Robert of Obazine had earlier given them when Peter Arnold had gone to Jerusalem. This was done in the hearing of John of Bordas, William cellerar, Peter Bernard, Deodatus, Pons of Vairac, Hugh of Vairac, Peter of Vairac, and Peter of Monpesler. . . . In the year of the Incarnation of the Lord, 1170, when Louis VII was king and Gerald was bishop of Limoges.[62]

46. COYROUX/OBAZINE, 1160–65: Gift before departure on pilgrimage

Raymond, viscount of Turenne, wishing to go to pray at the shrine of the blessed James the Apostle [at Compostela], made his testament. If he should die and does not have an heir from his wife, he donated to the monastery of Obazine all of his rights in Montanach with all its appurtenances. If he does have heirs, he will give the mansus of Ragaldas to that monastery. . . .[63]

47. COYROUX/OBAZINE, 1178: Viscountess Elizabeth and her son are guarantors

Geoffrey Toucheboeuf and his brothers Ugo, William, and Helyas gave into the hands of Abbot Robert and to the monastery of Obazine the meadow of les Junchières at Saint-Palladius with

---

[62] *Cartulaire d'Obazine*, no. 329 (1170–71).

[63] *Cartulaire d'Obazine*, no. 234 (1160–65).

the land pertaining to it. The abbot received Geoffrey into the benefits of Obazine and gave him 800 shillings. This was done in the hearing of Peter, prior, William, cellerar, Stephen Maurini, Gerald of Gourdon, Bernard of Corneil, Peter of Flaugiac, Bernard of Saint-Ardei, Stephen of Marcillac, Bernard of Cauforns, priest, and Stephen of Cantaloba, priest. Among those hearing were Elizabeth, viscountess of Turenne, and Boso, her son, who acted as guarantors. Other guarantors were William Robert of Chavanac, William his son, William Flucoall, and Peter of Faurgas the younger. Done in the year of the Incarnation of the Lord, 1178, when Louis VII was king and the bishop-elect of Limoges was Seebrand.[64]

48. COYROUX/OBAZINE, 1180:
Viscountess Elizabeth accepts a gift on behalf of Obazine

Peter of Martegnac and Geoffrey his brother gave to the monastery of Obazine all rights they had in the land and appurtenances of the grange of les Alys, and whatever their father and mother had earlier given to that monastery. They gave whatever they sought, justly or unjustly, not only in the appurtenances of les Alys, but in the bordaria of la Godelière, in the mansus of Rigalda, in Velmespol, Crauscher, Puy Usclat, and in all the lands that pertain to the grange of Baudran. They also gave to that monastery everything they had in all the lands that pertained to the grange of Saint-Palladius. All this was done into the hands of Elizabeth, viscountess of Turenne, who acted as guarantor, promising that the donors would no longer make any claims over the aforesaid lands. Then abbot Robert gave 130 shillings to Peter of Martegnac and Geoffrey his brother. Witnesses were William cellerar, Peter of Rigaut, Peter Faidit of Turenne, Gerald of

---

[64] *Cartulaire d'Obazine*, no. 495 (1178–79).

Ventadorn. In the year of the Incarnation of the Lord, 1181, when Philip II was king and Seebrand was bishop of Limoges.[65]

49. COYROUX/OBAZINE, 1191/92:
Reparations made for damages

Elizabeth, viscountess of Turenne, and Viscount Boso, her son, gave and conceded to God, the Blessed Mary, and the house of Obazine half of the mill of Tolvia. This was given in reparation for the damages that Obazine and its granges had suffered when that viscountess and her son had gone with their army to build the castle of Roche-de-Vic. This conveyance was done at the tower of Turenne into the hands of Gerald, bishop of Cahors, and Gerald, abbot of Obazine. Those listening were Peter of Rigaut, Roger of Corneil, Peter Faidit, Bernard Eustorgius of Nobiliac, and many others. This was done in the year of the Incarnation of the Lord, 1191, when Philip II was king of France, and Seebrand was bishop of Limoges.[66]

---

[65] *Cartulaire d'Obazine*, no. 590 (1181–82).

[66] *Cartulaire d'Obazine*, no. 779 (1191–92).

Le Tart and Jully

*T*raditional Cistercian histories have denied that the Order's early founders had anything to do with women. Indeed they deny the very existence of Cistercian nuns in the twelfth century. Cistercian nuns were thought to have been accepted into the Order only later in an irregular fashion because of pressure on its abbots by powerful patrons and the papacy.[67] However, although Cîteaux and its four earliest daughter-houses —la Ferté, Clairvaux, Pontigny, and Morimond—have been thought to have kept a strict distance from any involvement in the affairs of religious women in their earliest history, historians since the 1950s have been aware that the abbot of Cîteaux, Stephen Harding, had helped in the foundation of a house of religious women at le Tart in the 1120s (see nos. 50–51) and that these nuns at le Tart later would form a filiation of women's houses within the Order.

But the story of early nuns associated with the Cistercian reformers in whatever version should not stop with le Tart and its daughters. A parallel congregation of women's houses (usually treated as Benedictine rather than Cistercian, but being in spirit almost identical to the Cistercians) grew from a priory at Jully, which like Cîteaux once had been attached to Molesme. The Molesme cartulary, in fact, includes clear evidence that Jully was founded by religious women who once had been at Molesme itself (see nos. 52 and 53). The reform aims of the priory for

---

[67] For this version of events see Brigitte Degler-Spengler, "The Incorporation of Cistercian Nuns into the Order in the Twelfth and Thirteenth Century," *Hidden Springs* 3:1, 85–134; see also Constance H. Berman, "Were There Twelfth-Century Cistercian Nuns?" *Church History* 68 (1999), 324–64.

women at Jully, which had been founded from Molesme (no. 54), are remarkably similar to those usually associated with the Cistercians, for instance, with regard to what types of endowment they should have. Moreover, for Jully we have precise instructions from the founder, Milo, count of Bar, about how its more distant properties were to be administered for it by the monks of Molesme and how the nuns also should cultivate their own land near the abbey (see no. 54). As nos. 55–59 show, Jully had close ties to Clairvaux, and its first abbot, Bernard of Clairvaux, did support religious women. Indeed some of the nuns at Jully, like Humbelina (see no. 56), were his relatives, but Bernard also was active in accepting property for other nuns (nos. 57 and 58) and in assisting in their veiling (no. 59). Only later did Cistercian narratives leave out these parts of the story.

50. LE TART, 1125–36 : Tithes given in the parish of le Tart

Let everyone know that Galerius, priest of the village of le Tart, gave the tithes of that place to the church and holy nuns of le Tart with the approval of Guilencus, bishop of Langres, and Arnold of Dijon, his deacon, so that they all could be remembered in the prayers of the nuns. Witnesses for this gift were Hugh, duke of Burgundy, and Matilda, his wife, and Eudes, Hugh, Henry, and Raymond, their sons; Aymo Rufus; William of Marrivo and Hugh Danduo, his paternal uncle.

I, Hugh, duke of Burgundy, announce by these words my confirmation of this gift made to God, Saint Mary, and the holy nuns of le Tart, so that they may have it as long as their community continues to exist. Moreover, with the consent of my wife and my sons, Eudes, Hugh, and Raymond, I also give the holding or lordship called Marmot with its appendices, for the nuns of le Tart to cultivate and to do whatever they need there. Witnesses were Gosbert viscount, Bartholomew of Fountains, Gosbert of Granceio, Haimo Rufus, William of Marrivo, William of Orgeuil, Eudes Caynus, and Peter Gaberons.[68]

51. LE TART, 1147: Pope Eugenius III grants tithe privileges to le Tart

Eugenius, servant of the servants of God, to my dear in Christ daughter, Elizabeth, abbess of le Tart, and to the sisters there perpetually professing the regular life now and in the future. Because it is desirable that things concerning the religious life and the welfare of souls be of the first concern to the ministers of the Church, we have responded to your request, and have taken you, my dear in Christ daughter, and your community under the divine

---

[68] *Patrologiae Latinae Cursus Completus*, ed. J.-P. Migne, vol. 185 (Paris, 1879), cols. 1410–11.

hand of blessed Peter and under our own protection by the privilege of these words. By the help of God we establish that whatever possessions or goods you possess, justly and canonically, at present or in future, by papal concessions, the largess of kings or princes, the gifts of the faithful, or by other means, remain in your hands and those of your successors. In particular the properties that you now have at the following places: namely, the place called le Tart, the place called Marmot with its appurtenances, usage in all the woods of Villers, the grange of Lamblent with its appurtenances which Humbert of Bissey and Peter Major and his heirs gave you with the consent of Hugh of Belmont, in whose jurisdiction it is located, as well as full usage rights, in fields, woods, pastures. We also confirm the tithes conveyed to you by those who claimed their possession before the dedication of that grange. Furthermore, we declare that no one should presume to exact tithes from you on the produce of the labor of your own hands or your management, or from the feeding and increase of your animals. . . .[69]

52. MOLESME, 1075–85: Lesselin of Maisey-le-Duc and his sister enter Molesme

Lesselin of Maisey put on the holy religious habit and gave the church of Campaniola and everything pertaining to it to God, Saint Mary, and the church of Molesme. He did this as much for himself as for his sister, Odeline, at the time when she converted to living the religious life at Molesme. . . .[70]

---

[69] *PL*, ed. Migne, vol. 180, cols. 1199–1200.

[70] *Cartulaires de l'abbaye de Molesme, ancien diocèse de Langres, 916–1250: recueil de documents sur le nord de la Bourgogne et le midi de la Champagne,* ed. Jacques Laurent, vol. 1 (Paris, 1907), no. 135.

53. MOLESME, ca. 1075: Entrance of Elizabeth and her son

Elizabeth, sister of Hugh of Belmont, made a gift to the church of Molesme. She came with a single young son named Eudes to the church of Molesme and, wishing to relinquish secular life, gave herself and her son so that they could take religious habits and remain assiduously serving God and his holy mother Mary along with the brothers of that house. And thus this woman entered that place where she henceforth lived a religious life with other women who, like her, had given up the cares of the secular life.[71]

54. JULLY, ca. 1115: Gift of the site at Jully

I, Milo, count of Bar, warned by an all-knowing God and girded in the armor and words of the Christian faith, wish to make manifest by the present words the gift which I made to the church of Molesme, that is, the gift of the property at Jully. Hoping that at the end of time a merciful God will judge that I have made recompense for at least a portion of my sins, and thus providing for the health of my own soul and that of the souls of my relatives—alive or dead—and with the confirmation of my wife and my sons, I transfer to God, his saintly mother, Mary, and to Molesme, the castle of Jully with all its appurtenances in the parish of Saint-Andrew, the castle which once belonged to my ancestor, Count Milo, to found there a community of religious women where once there were only evil spirits. I praise and confirm to the church of Molesme any lordship I have. . . . So that the nuns at the castle of Jully can lead the most religious lives possible and be able to serve God quietly at that place under the guidance of the abbot of Molesme, I assign management of the resources for the food and other necessities of those nuns and lay-

---

[71] *Cartulaires de Molesme*, ed. Laurent, vol. 1, no. 79.

sisters to Lord Guy, abbot, and the community of Molesme. Thus, the nuns' property will be held for them by Molesme, but in addition to the produce from lands worked and cultivated by their oxen, these women will hold in common whatever is given to them by the abbot of Molesme for their food and clothing. Their endowment should include neither serfs nor their wives, nor churches, tithes, or manors, and whatever is given to the nuns ought to be kept by the church of Molesme for them. Jully will have direct control only of its movable goods. Molesme should provide the nuns of Jully enough land to cultivate with their own plows. The nuns of Jully should follow the Lord under a regime in which four monks sent from the abbey of Molesme will be responsible for the care of the bodies and souls of the nuns, and will protect them from all harm and keep them from needing to leave their enclosure to undertake business. . . .[72]

55. JULLY, 1128: Aanolz, wife of Walter of Roche, becomes a nun at Jully

May all at present and in future note that Walter of la Roche held an annuity or money-fief worth 10 pounds from Thibault, count of Blois. This amount was paid annually from the proceeds of the fairs of Bar. After Walter died, his wife Aanolz left the world to enter Jully as a lay-sister and gave that annuity to the nuns, and gave that gift into the hands of Prior Peter at the chapter of Jully in front of the entire community. This most generous gift Aanolz confirmed, conceded, and transferred with her own hand. Present were Ranier, brother of Walter of la Roche; and Bernard of Montbar, stepson of said Walter, who conceded and confirmed whatever pertained to him from that gift. Also present was

---

[72] *Histoire du prieuré de Jully avec pièces justificatives*, par l'abbé Jobin (Paris, 1881), no. 1 (c.1115). Found also in *PL*, ed. Migne, vol. 195, cols. 1408–09.

Bernard, abbot of Clairvaux, with three of his monks: Godfrey, Gerald, and Ranier; and three monks from Molesme: Robert, Guy, and Eudes.

Witnesses for these things were Bouchard, bishop of Meaux, Guy, count of Bar, Gaufridus of Joinville, Reginald of Lezinnes, Hugh of Lisoio, Goscelin of Dammartin, Gauthier of Bernon, Adam, viscount of Bar, Fulk Amator of Troyes, Goscelin of Isle, Bernard of Montbar, and Raynaud, viscount of Rourmont. Nivard confirmed all this along with Rainier his brother, for which confirmation the witnesses were Bernard of Montbar and Tescelin Pultariensis. This gift was confirmed and praised by Guilencus, bishop of Langres, at Bar-sur-Aube. Witnesses for this confirmation were Bernard of Clairvaux, Gerald his brother, and Gerald, archdeacon of Langres.

This was also confirmed and conceded by two young girls, Gertrude and Agnes, the daughters of said Walter. For this gift witnesses were Gerald, servant of the count of Bar; Robert Provost, son of Rabaudus; Guiard, son of Walter; Eudes Rufus; and Hugh of Porta. This gift was done on Thursday, March 28, at Jully. On the following Thursday the charter was written. This was done when Guilencus was bishop of Langres, and Louis VI was king, in the year of the Incarnation of the Lord, 1128. This gift was confirmed by Matilda, countess of Blois, and conceded at Castle Theodoric in the presence of Count Thibault, her husband; Andrew of Bauriment; Guy, a monk of Jully; Gaubert chaplain; Letard chaplain; Charvaillano, chamberlain of the countess; and Lady Elisendis of Meaux.[73]

---

[73] *Histoire de Jully*, no. 3 (1128).

56. JULLY, MAY 1, 1133: Humbelina, sister of Bernard of Clairvaux, gives tithes

Because the masters of the holy Church ought to provide for the poor in Christ and by ecclesiastical authority defend the endowment of those poor, we therefore with these present words, lest by forgetfulness or any other reason these possessions of the servants of God come under dispute, commend to the memory of those in the future the gift of the tithes of the church of Saint-Leo which Humbelina, wife of Ansericus of Cacennac, made to the holy nuns of Jully with the confirmation of her husband. Thus Humbelina, providing for the health of her own as well as that of her ancestors' souls, gave to God, the Blessed Mary, and the holy nuns of Jully whatever she had in the tithes of that villa which is called Saint-Leo, and everything she has there, keeping nothing for herself or her successors in that villa, except her men. She made this gift in the hand of bishop Hato of Troyes, in whose jurisdiction it is located. That bishop confirmed this and conceded to Jully any residual part of the tithes which those holy nuns may henceforth acquire in that villa. Moreover, that this may remain valid, he bestowed on it the confirmation of his seal, with the appropriate witnesses and with the assistance of the venerable bishops Lord Godfrey of Chartres and Lord Bouchard of Meaux, of Guy, abbot of Trois-Fontaines, Godfrey, prior of Clairvaux, and Gerald, brother of the abbot of Clairvaux. Witnesses were Guy Ruf of Fonteto, Bencilinus of Malay, Rainaldus Clarellus, Arraudus of Laniis, Gautier Provost, Peter Govins, and Guineman. Jacob, son of Lady Humbelina, confirmed this before the witnesses listed. Done in the year of the Incarnation of our Lord, 1133, indiction 11, concurrent 6, epact twelve, May 1, at the bishop's house.[74]

---

[74] *Histoire de Jully*, no. 6 (1133).

57. JULLY, BEFORE 1137: Bernard of Clairvaux transfers property from Clairvaux to Jully

In the name of God, I, Bernard, abbot of Clairvaux, wish to have noted that Fulk of Bar and Rexis his wife gave their house at Bar to me in the presence of our brothers Wido and Gerald, and by testimony of the faithful men of Bar, Gibert provost there, Wido Asinarii, Wido, son of Genterii, Odo Rufi, Roland the younger, Robert his son, and Aluisus. Retaining nothing in my hands, I then freely gave that same house to the church of Jully and its nuns there, with confirmation by our brothers Wido and Gerald, as witnessed by the men named above. In order that the church of Jully possess this house freely and quietly, I have had this charter made and confirmed it with my seal.[75]

58. JULLY, 1142: Veiling of nuns at Jully by Bernard of Clairvaux

I, Godfrey, by the grace of God, bishop of Langres, make known to present and future readers that at the request of Lord Andrew of Bitumenoid and his son Guy, I went to the house of Jully. There, along with Lord Bernard, abbot of Clairvaux, I solemnly received the two daughters of Andrew, named Matilda and Halvidis, into the community of holy nuns there. Then Andrew and Guy, for themselves and for the relief of their souls, gave 40 shillings in cens from their income in the villa called Jouy, which are to be paid at the feast of Saint Rémy. . . . In the year of the Incarnation of the Lord, 1142.[76]

---

[75] *Histoire de Jully*, no. 7 (before 1137).

[76] *PL*, ed. Migne, vol. 185, col. 1409.

59. JULLY, ca. 1142: Bernard of Clairvaux receives a donation for one of Jully's daughter-houses

I, Godfrey, bishop of Langres, notify everyone at present or in future that when that daughter-house of Jully [Pré] was built, Garnier of Subernum, with the confirmation of his sons, Hervé and Guy, gave alms to that house of Pré or Prélongue into the hands of the venerable abbot Bernard of Clairvaux and into my own. Those donors also gave woodland usage throughout their lands for taking construction materials, firewood, for pasture, and for all the necessities of that house. They give fishing rights in their streams and pasture rights throughout their lands. Bartholomew, brother of Garnier, himself also made a gift like this, and confirmed the gifts made by his brother. Warner of Age and Guy Garcilas made the same concession of usage rights in their lands. All this was confirmed much later at Jully in our presence. Witnesses to these things were the venerable abbot of Saint-Benigne, Albert of Saint-Stephen of Dijon, Lambert, canon and sacristan of the church of Langres, and Robert, deacon of Subernum, and Guiard of Saint-Burri.[77]

---

[77] *PL*, 185, cols. 1408–09.

Part III

Statistical Sources

Statistical Sources

℘ t has been assumed in traditional treatments that nuns were invariably poor and illiterate. They produced no literary or theological masterpieces, nor did they even keep good records about their property. But recent study of their documents has shown that nuns were good record-keepers, possibly because their sources of income were too limited to be neglected. Communities of nuns often compiled lists of cash income or other account books to aid in their management of property, and we find them speaking of "our rents" and "the payments we owe." They were told to do such accounting by their visitors (see no. 65 below). But we are apt to read such strictures about record-keeping as reflecting poverty. Today we recognize that, as in some marriages, complaints of improper resource management are a way of acting out conflicts about other things; when we consider the "hothouse atmosphere" of life in any religious community— with nuns or monks who entered at different ages from different backgrounds and with different expectations of what "poverty" entailed—it is obvious that accusations of improper account-keeping or about the uses to which property was being put could easily arise. This may have been the case with regard to the property that Blanche of Paciac had brought to Saint-Antoine; see no. 15 above.

The accounts excerpted here come from several of the largest and wealthiest houses of Cistercian nuns in France. As may be seen even from the excerpts of its 1260s rent roll (no. 60), the abbey of Port-Royal held a range of properties in both Paris and the rural areas in the direction of Chartres. The rent-roll from Saint-Antoine (no. 61), from which I have included a short portion, is found in that abbey's medieval cartulary; it is written in old French rather than Latin, possibly indicating that nuns not literate in Latin undertook its compilation; the context suggests it comes from 1344. The third excerpt (no. 62) comes from the account book made by the Templar master, Richard, who was "foreman" for Queen Blanche of Castile in the construction of the church and abbey for Cistercian women at Maubuisson. The existence of this account book confirms that in some cases a patron would construct an entire monastic complex and church before settling nuns there—nuns sent in this case from Saint-Antoine. In many ways this volume is frustrating to use because it is a running account, with occasional totals reported to the queen three times a year. It shows much about prices and necessary materials, but unlike the other two accounts excerpted here, Blanche's account book shows no systematization of expenses or receipts into categories. Expenditures were recorded when they came up, rather than being in any way separated out by categories. These account books provide us with indirect evidence about nuns' property management and more direct evidence about their accounting skills.

60. PORT-ROYAL, ca. 1260:
Excerpts from a rent roll for Port-Royal

1. These rents and money payments we collect at the feast of Saint Rémy:

> At Karrerias we have 100 shillings from the gift of Lady Marguerite, lady of Narbonne, for her daughter.
>
> From the gift of Master Simon of Gif, 31 shillings at Gif.
>
> In the cens of Gometh-le-Chastel, 20 shillings from Lord Guy of Montfort.
>
> In the cens of Romerville, 20 shillings from Lady Clemencie of Plessy.

In the cens of Plessy, 10 shillings from Lord Milo, knight there.

In the cens of Marches, 10 shillings and 12 shillings for wine from the gift made by Lord Hugh, knight there, for his daughter.

From the gift of Peter of Chouses, 6 pounds of Chartres at Provetport paid at two dates: 60 shillings at the feast of Saint Rémy, and 60 on Brandon Sunday.

At Aulnay, 15 shillings in cens: 5 at Saint Rémy, 5 at the Purification of the Blessed Virgin, and 5 at the feast of the Assumption of our Lord. . . .

2. *These rents of cash we collect at various terms:*
   At Meulan, 30 pounds from the gift of Lord Matthew of Montmorency who was the lord of Marly, and from the sons of said Matthew, Lord Bouchard and Lord Matthew, who were the most dear founders of the abbey of Port-Royal.

   From the gift of Sedilia of Noicy, 8 pounds rent with another 30 pounds: that is 9.5 pounds money paid on each of the following dates: March 1, June 1, September 1, and December 1.

   Also at the Châtellet of Paris from the gift of the Lord King of France, 45 pounds, 12 shillings, and 6 pennies at three dates. . . .

3. *Also we have:*
   At Saint-Genevieve in Paris, 12 pounds annual rent from Lady Marguerite, lady of Narbonne, 4 pounds to be paid at each of three dates: in the week of All Saints, of Christmas, and Easter.

   Also at Paris we have 12 shillings annual rent which Bertald Asselin agreed to pay in the week after Palm Sunday.

Also at Paris at a certain window over the Grand Pont, 10 shillings annual rent from Petronilla of Auvergne in the week after Palm Sunday.

Also at Tornenfuic, 29 shillings on the feast of All Souls.

Also at Galardon, 50 shillings annual rent to be paid us in the week of All Saints from the gift of Lord Bouchard the Younger of Marly from his provostry of Galardon.

Also we have 5 shillings money in cens from Lord Hugh of Bordis or Lord Simon Bagot to be paid at Bordas at the winter feast of Saint Martin.

Also at Galardon, 6 pounds of Chartres annual rent from a gift from Adam and Philip, lords of Galardon, for their sister Amicia, payable in the fortnight of Christmas from their provostry.

At Verneuil, 10 shillings annually owed at Christmas by the incumbent of Saint-Martin.

At Chartres from the gift of John of Colrouge, 4 pounds: half to be paid at Christmas, half at the feast of Saint John the Baptist.

Also at Chartres, 4 pounds from the gift of Lord Bouchard the Elder to be paid at the feast of the Purification of the Lord.

Also at Montlhéry, 100 shillings annual rent for as long as Arnold the Butcher and Flora his wife live: half to be paid at Christmas, half at Saint John the Baptist.

At la Ferté, 15 pounds money from the gift of Lord Philip of Montfort for his sister Petronilla, 100 shillings of which are paid on Brandon Sunday, and 10 pounds on the feast of Saint John the Baptist. . . .[78]

---

[78] *Cartulaire de Port-Royal*, 15–24.

61. SAINT-ANTOINE, **ca. 1344: Excerpts from a rent list of Parisian properties**

On the Petit Pont:
For the house of P. the Vaileress, 13 shillings quarterly.

For the house of the late Joan la Bardelle, 16 shillings, 3 pennies quarterly.

On the street of the Jewery:
For the house of the late Belle Alice, 6 shillings, 8 pennies quarterly.

For that of the late Mary called Assis, 60 shillings quarterly.

For that of the late Peter Perudome, 20 shillings quarterly.

For that of Anchiel the Laudent, 60 shillings quarterly.

For that of the late John of Bellay, who was the agent for Tiron, 20 shillings at Christmas and at the feast of Saint John.

For that of Master John Pastourel, 9 pounds quarterly.

At the Port Baudoet:
For the house of the late B. Mor, 14 shillings, 4 pennies, and an obol quarterly.

For the house of John the Liguier, 60 shillings quarterly.

For the house of John des Greucz, 7 pounds, 10 shillings quarterly.

For the house of Gila of la Bar, 7 pounds, 18 shillings

For the house of Robert Enguignant, 70 shillings quarterly.

On the street of the nuns of Yerres:
For the house of the late Gila of Roissy, 17 shillings quarterly.

For the house of the late John the Finere, 100 shillings quarterly. . . .

Near the cemetery of Saint John:

For the house of Eraves the Mayor, 60 shillings quarterly.

For the house of the late Gila Bardy, 57 shillings quarterly.

For that of the late Liurs the Master, 15 shillings quarterly.

For the house of Peter, 30 shillings quarterly.

For the house of Jacques Marcel, 50 shillings quarterly.

For the house of Peter Bagau, 40 shillings quarterly.

On the street of the Gardens:

For the house of Richard of Teneloe, 38 shillings quarterly.

For the house of the late Hoderel, 20 shillings quarterly.

For the house of the late Adam Pitancier, 10 shillings quarterly.

Also 9 pounds and 4 shillings of Longuy Leander of Severius Scotus.

In the little street of the Temple, 40 shillings of Tours from the late Sabiau of Blondelle.

For the house of the late John Roussel in the Rue Sainte-Croix from Master Peter the Miller, 25 shillings quarterly.

For the house at the end of the street called the Old Street of the Temple, 20 shillings quarterly.

On the little street of the Weavers:

For the house of John of Paray, 4 pounds.

For the house of the late Estie of Torcy, 70 shillings quarterly.

For the house of the bells, 5 shillings at Saint John. . . .

From the abbess of Villars, 5 shillings at Saint John.

For the house of the late Leannus the Cochitur, 3 shillings at Saint John.

For the house of Singuelou the Bonin Greignon, 20 shillings quarterly.

For the house of the grandfather of Gila Ruyel, in the March term, 40 shillings quarterly.

For the house of Robert Veuvillet in front of Saint-John of the Grève, 40 shillings quarterly.

At the Place Grève:

For the house of Tromet, 6 pounds quarterly.

For the house of Daur Mos, 60 shillings quarterly.

In the Tannery:

For the house of the late John of Lan, 40 shillings quarterly.

For that of Robert or Peter Loc, 40 shillings quarterly.

For that of Master John Ferrartz, 55 shillings, 5 pennies quarterly.

For the Courcel of Robert of Toie, 16 shillings quarterly.

For the house of the late Martin Dauchuguis, 20 shillings at Christmas and at the feast of Saint John.

For the house of the late John Mallet, 40 shillings quarterly.

For the house of Peter Foussel, 40 shillings quarterly. . . .

In the Marais:

For the house of John of Tel, 6 shillings, 6 pennies quarterly.

For the house of John the Ancre, 16 shillings quarterly.

For that of the late Robert of Bonnefort, 75 shillings quarterly.

In the Petit Marais:

For the house of Peter Lambert, 55 shillings, 5 pennies paid twice annually.

For the house of the late Gila of Laymasi, 9 shillings, 9 pennies twice annually.

For the house of Jacques of Bouliz, 52 shillings, 8 pennies twice annually.

For the house of Menrie, 5 shillings twice annually.

For the house of the late Gila Bruia, 10 shillings twice annually.

For the house of Pons Gathier of Nesle, 44 shillings, 2 pennies quarterly. . . .

On the great street of Saint-Denis:

For the house of Nicolas le Laran, 11 shillings quarterly.

For the house of John Rouce, priest of Saint-Magloire, 20 shillings quarterly.

For the house of the late Ancre of Chamblys, 4 shillings, 3 pennies twice a year.

For the house of the late Peter of the Queue, 9 shillings, 4 pennies twice a year.

At les Halles of Paris:

For the house of the late Nicholas Burgat, 9 pounds quarterly.

For the house of the Cornaille, 12 pounds, 5 shillings, 7 pennies quarterly.

For the house of the late John Thomas, 7 pounds, 10 shillings quarterly.

For the house of the late Robert of Dieppe, 43 shillings quarterly.

For the house of Robert of the Lateve, 10 pounds quarterly.

For the house of the late Henry of the Hague, 61 shillings, 2 pennies quarterly.

For the house of Nicholas de Soissons, located on the Street of the Poers, 8 pounds, 10 shillings quarterly.

For the house of the late Lautoice Presficie adjoining the Bicler et chausee du Molouest, 100 shillings quarterly.

For the house of Raoul the Charron, 4 pounds, 5 shillings quarterly.

For the house of Parram Madame, 20 shillings quarterly.

For our large house in the Halles, 20 pounds quarterly. . . .

Near the Châtellet:

For the house of William of Meaux, 100 shillings due at Christmas.

For the stable of Robert Lestanaur, 100 shillings quarterly.

For the large palace of M. Mail, 30 shillings quarterly. . . .

In the street of the Harp:

For the house of Adam the Crucifer, 50 shillings quarterly.

For the house of the heirs of Droignat, 100 shillings quarterly.

For the house of the late Gila Lemarit, 100 shillings quarterly.

For the house of B. Pelletier, in the street of the Skinners, 50 shillings, quarterly.

On the great street of Saint-James:

For the house of Lisa Gelco opposite Saint-Leonard's enclosure, 7 pounds, 10 shillings quarterly.

For the house of Elnias of Claques, 40 shillings quarterly.

For the house of E. the Barber and William the Tanner, 7 pounds, 10 shillings quarterly.

For the house of Peter the Bailliff, 4 pounds, 5 shillings quarterly.

For the house of Romero Calent, 10 shillings quarterly.

For the house of Gilet the Moustardier, 7 pounds, 10 shillings quarterly. . . .

Total for all rents from houses in Paris, 612 pounds, 10 shillings, 8 pennies for this year for both the ground rent and all other appurtenances leased.[79]

62. MAUBUISSON, 1237: Receipts and expenditures reported to Queen Blanche of Castile

For 1237 was received:

From the citizens of Pontoise by Master Theonis, 3 pounds.

Into the hand of Master Peter of Lyre, 3 pounds.

Into the hand of Brother Giles, treasurer of the Temple in Paris, for two terms, 1,000 pounds.

Also in that same year at the feast of the blessed Martin in Paris into the hand of Brother Gilon, 4 pounds.

Also 4 pounds at Pontoise into the hand of Compagnon on the Friday of the week when "Lift up mine eyes" is sung.[80]

Also at Pontoise in 1237, on the first Thursday before the Lord's Ascension by Brother Guiot, 3 pounds.

Also received into the hand of Brother Gilon to pay John Morier for a portion of the masonry for the dormitory, 224 pounds, 14 shillings, 6 pennies. . . .

Master Richard, and brother Gilon accounted for the above on the Monday after the feast of the Ascension: The total was 2,939 pounds, 14 shillings, six pennies.

---

[79] Paris, A.N. LL1595, fols. 87r–90r.

[80] Probably a reference to Psalm 122/123 sung on All Souls Day (November 2).

These amounts were paid out by Master Richard:
To Brother Gerald for constructing the fountain, 219 pounds, 7 shillings, 9 pennies.

To Master Robert, carpenter, for rafters and roof beams for the dormitory, 97 pounds.

For the rafters, and roof beams for the chapel, 13 pounds, 16 shillings, 2 pennies.

For the ironwork for doors, and windows, 13 pounds, 4 shillings, 9 pennies.

For other ironwork, 17 pounds, 10 shillings.

To John Moriers, for masonry for the dormitory, 224 pounds, 14 shillings, 6 pennies.

For the masonry of the chapel, and for heating, 42 pounds, 10 shillings.

For glass for the chapel, 12 pounds, 10 shillings.

For one heavy cable, and other ropes, 12 pounds, 80 shillings.

For floor-tiles for the dormitory, 73 pounds.

For glass-making, 60 shillings.

To the gardener for manure, 75 shillings, 4 pennies.

For the period up to the feast of the blessed Andrew, 1237, the total expended was 1432 pounds, 16 shillings, and 5 pennies . . . .

This was detailed when Master Richard gave accounts to the Lady Queen:
For the fountain, 64 shillings, 6 pennies.

For lead, 22 shillings, 8 pennies.

To Master Robert, carpenter, 9 pounds, 19 shillings.

To make the gardens, 37 shillings, 6 pennies.

For the work of gardeners, 20 shillings, 4 pennies.

To glass-makers in Pontoise, 40 shillings.

To those making claims for paving, 25 pounds.

To the tilers, 18 pounds, 5 shillings, 8 pennies.

To John Morier for one wall of masonry for the dormitory, 60 pounds.

To Henry Rocheron for masonry for the priest's house, 52 pounds, 2 shillings, 6 pennies.

To William of la Broce, for masonry of cloister walls, wood panels, and grillwork, 78 pounds, 5 shillings.

For 250 pieces of cut stone, 6 pounds.

For tiles, 23 pounds.

To Robert of Rouen for roof tiles, 12 pounds, 100 shillings.

To the same Robert for little tiles, 26 pounds, 10 shillings.

To Walter of Vieux Conches for 23,200 pieces of oak paneling, 59 pounds, 8 shillings.

For tiles and roofing squares, 10 pounds.

For roof tiles for the infirmary and cloister, masonry in the kitchen, and other small masonry jobs, 78 pounds, 5 shillings.

For 41,000 flooring boards, 35 pounds, 4 shillings.

For transport of the aforesaid, 44 pounds, 5 shillings.

For unloading of the aforesaid, 44 shillings.

For 503 pieces of cut stone for frames for the windows and six doors, 12 pounds, 2 shillings, 3 pennies.

For stone framing of one large doorway six feet wide, 40 shillings.

For 250 tiles, 50 shillings.

For 1000 panels of beech-wood, 28 shillings.

For 26 pieces of cut stone, 16 shillings.

For 4000 floor boards, 67 shillings, 2 pennies.

To Robert Racine for transport of the aforesaid, 7 pounds.

For the period from the feast of the blessed Andrew [1236] *up to the feast of All Saints, 1237, the total expended was: 60,080 pounds, 62 shillings, 7 pennies.*[81]

---

[81] Pontoise, A.D. Val d'Oise, H 58, no. 4, Registre de Maubuisson, parchment codex entitled "Achatz et heritages"; partially published in Henri de l'Épinois, "Comptes relatifs à la fondation de l'abbaye de Maubuisson, d'après les originaux des archives de Versailles," *Bibliothèque de l'École de Chartes* 1 (1858), 550–69.

Part IV

Narrative and Normative Sources

Narrative and Normative Sources

*U*ntil recently, historians describing nuns in the Middle Ages were apt to cite medieval chroniclers whose narratives depicted Cistercian nuns or to seek out normative sources such as episcopal visitation records. Most often nuns were left out of the story altogether, so what is available is often snippets of evidence taken out of context. Such chronicles provide a different view from the charter evidence whose existence depended on an administrative need—to record land conveyances. Such narrative sources were almost entirely written by ecclesiastical men—priests and monks who found it difficult to be open-minded about religious women. All women posed a threat to their clerical chastity, and religious women were demanding of their time and efforts. These writers, even when they praised Cistercian women, described them in distorted ways. Indeed, the first two narrative examples found here (nos. 63 and 64) have a history of being misread by historians intent on using them to prove that there were no Cistercian nuns until after the passing of the "Golden Age" of the Order's earliest history.

But also problematic are normative sources, such as the constitutions established for the nuns of Nun Coton upon the visit of a bishop of Lincoln to that community in the early thirteenth century (no. 65), or the notes generated at the Cistercian General Chapter meeting of 1243 (no. 66) about rebelliousness on the part of nuns that resulted from attempts by abbots to enforce rather draconian measures. Such evidence, when taken out of context, is too easily read as evidence for specifically female offenses against enclosure and good management.

The earliest mention of Cistercian nuns from an external witness is found in Herman of Tournai's book about religious reform, called *The Miracles of Saint-Mary of Laon*. Two relevant passages are included below (no. 63). The first (section a) has been interpreted as evidence that the most famous twelfth-century Cistercian, Bernard of Clairvaux, disapproved of nuns in contrast to his rival Norbert, founder of the Praemonstratensians. But a more careful reading of Herman's report suggests that separate religious houses, rather than hostility to women *per se*, was what differentiated Cistercian from Praemonstratensian reformers according to Herman. This is borne out in the second relevant section of Herman's tract (section b). There he speaks of the early house of Cistercian nuns near Laon, at Montreuil-les-Dames.

The second description (no. 64) is one of the most-cited descriptions of religious orders from the early thirteenth century, that of the Paris university-trained theologian, James of Vitry, who wrote a tract called the *Historia occidentalis*. Each chapter of this volume is a description, often in caricature, of a different group. The description of Cistercian women in his tract is quoted often, but we must not conclude that James is saying that there were no Cistercian nuns before the Praemonstratensian canons tried to jettison the sisters from their midst.

A visitation of the abbey of nuns at Nun Coton in England (no. 65) reveals some of the issues of concern to bishops visiting houses of nuns, including appropriate size and record-keeping. This visitation was done by Hugh of Wells, bishop of Lincoln from 1209–35, although it earlier was ascribed to bishop Saint Hugh of Lincoln (1186–1200). Concerns about record-keeping, about the size of the house, and about the poverty of the inhabitants are those of the thirteenth-century program of regularization of nuns that we associate with Pope Gregory IX (1227–41) and his successors.

Notes preserved from the 1243 General Chapter meeting (no. 66) show some women's communities refusing to abide by new rules that the abbots in 1242 had decided to impose on houses of nuns. I have extracted only items concerning control of nuns;

there are others in the same year concerning monks, and it is clearly not just the nuns who created problems. But the incidents in 1243 show the nuns outraged by specific recent efforts made toward regularization of nuns within the Order, efforts from which the abbots would back down. But the trends towards regularization of religious women more generally would continue—right up to the issuance in 1298 of the papal bull *Periculoso*. Women's communities that once had possessed the freedom and flexibility to choose their own visitors would be attached directly to neighboring houses of men, and earlier ties among houses of women would be broken. Indeed, by the end of the thirteenth century even the annual assembly of abbesses at le Tart was suspended.

63. HERMAN OF TOURNAI, CANON OF LAON, ca. 1150:
Two comments on Cistercian women

a. The monastery of Cîteaux receives only men, whereas Lord Norbert has allowed that not only the male gender but the female as well be accepted in religious conversion; thus we see that the harsher and stricter conversions of women rather than those of men alone are seen in Norbert's monasteries.[82]

b. There were also eight new monasteries constructed by Lord Bartholomew in his diocese of Laon. Of these three were of monks from Clairvaux and five were of clerics from Prémontré thus totaling eight male reform houses. Also Lord Bartholomew ordained that there be added a ninth abbey, which brought the number of new communities in his diocese up to the number of the nine virtues of the order of the angels.

---

[82] *De miraculis sanctae Mariae Laudunensis* of Herman of Tournay, in *PL*, ed. Migne, vol. 156: 962–1018, col. 996.

This new monastery was for the feminine gender and was founded at a place called Montreuil. There he named as abbess an extremely religious girl named Guibergis. In no other part of the world has it ever been read in books or heard by ears of such women as lived at this abbey. . . . They lived according to the *ordo* of Cîteaux, which is difficult even for men . . . , working hard not at sewing and weaving—the usual women's work—but at harvesting the fields, pulling up brush, uprooting the forest, and working their fields, living with only wild beasts as their neighbors. Seeking their food in silence, these women imitated in all things the lives of the monks of Clairvaux, a clear sign from the Lord that all is possible for those who believe.[83]

64. JAMES OF VITRY, ca. 1220: Increase in Cistercian women

The reverend religious men of the Praemonstratensian Order, wisely attending to the assertions of experts within their own family that it was burdensome and dangerous to guard such charges, decided that they should henceforth not receive women into the houses of their Order. Thereafter abbeys of nuns of the Cistercian Order multiplied like the stars of heaven and increased enormously, blessed by God as it is said, "Increase and be multiplied and replenish the sky."[84]

---

[83] Ibid., cols. 1001–02.

[84] The *"Historia Occidentalis" of Jacques de Vitry. A Critical Edition*, ed. John Frederick Hinnebusch (Fribourg, 1972), 6 (for date), 117 (for text).

65. HUGH, BISHOP OF LINCOLN, 1209–35:
Visit to Nun Coton and Institutes

Hugh, bishop of Lincoln sends greetings in the Lord to all the faithful of Christ who see these present words. When we went to visit the community of servants of Christ at Nun Coton in order to conduct a visitation, as we are obliged to do because of our office as bishop, being anxious to apply assistance to those nuns, we made the following corrections:

1. Finding that the number of nuns was greater than were the facilities of the house to support them, we established with the consent of the master, prioress, and community, that given the restrictions of their endowment, the community of nuns and other sisters henceforth should not exceed the number of thirty, with twelve lay-brothers to do the work on the rural properties. In addition there will be a master chaplain to conduct the divine service with the assistance of two other chaplains to whom he will depute some of the duties. No new religious inhabitants should be admitted to said house until the present community has decreased in size to below the established maximum, except in cases of the obvious utility of the house and then with special license of the bishop.

2. The seal of the house should be kept in the custody of the master, prioress, and a wise nun elected by the entire community, each of whom should have one of the three keys to it. No documents should be sealed without the knowledge of the entire chapter of nuns, or at least of its wiser part. All rents, renewals, and annual payments of whatever kind ought to be written down. The prioress, sub-prioress, and four other prudent nuns elected by the chapter should have custody of the accounts, handing over to the master and provosts of the house any cash or other income. The master should record under his seal in front of those six nuns what they have given to him.

They will record the expenditures of the house and how much was used for its works, and the rest will be placed in the hands and under the seal of the master. Each month these six nuns will make up the accounts for the expenditures of the house.

3. Whatever properties are brought to that house at the time of the profession of a nun should not be the property of any individual in that house. Indeed, no one, once having taken the religious habit, should presume to have any property of her own, but all the property of the nuns should be held in common among them.

4. The nuns, chaplains, brothers, and sisters, as well as any guests, will have the same type of bread to eat and the same drink, except that special delicacies should be provided to the sick when possible, if they are necessary.

5. Because the frequenting of the house by seculars upsets the quiet of the religious life, we prohibit that any man or woman wearing the garb of seculars be received, as has been the practice in the said house, except to stay overnight as justified in hospitality to travelers.

6. Let no one, either male or female, whether a secular person or one professing the religious life, coming from anywhere, be allowed to talk alone with the nuns, but only under observation by an honest witness who takes care for any suspicion of evil, and only when permission has been obtained, following the rules of those who preside.

7. Because it is inappropriate in every way for religious men and women, but particularly the female sex, to wander around or travel, we establish that no lay-sister or nun may live at a grange in order to see to the raising of animals or for any other reason. Also the nuns should never be sent outside to visit neighbors or relatives because of their own desire, or for whatever reason or means, without the special license of the master and prioress, and because of a great and perceived necessity.

8. Because the sin of simony leads many into errors and continually prevents provisions made for the health of souls, we strictly prohibit any man or woman to be received there by any contract for money or any other temporal thing.

We command that all the things written here be firmly observed in all details perpetually by both sexes serving God in said house under threat of punishment by excommunication.[85]

66. GENERAL CHAPTER OF CÎTEAUX, 1243:
Notes concerning specific houses of nuns

Item 55: The complaint of the abbot of Clairefontaine against the abbess of Droitevaux was committed to the abbots of Bethune and Acey for settlement.

Item 56: The complaint of the abbot of les Vaux-de-Cernay against the abbess of Saint-Antoine-des-Champs of Paris was placed in the hands of the abbots of Beaubec in the diocese of Rouen and Barbeaux in the diocese of Meaux.

Item 57: The complaint of the abbot of Val-Saint-Lambert against the abbess of Beaufays was placed in the hands of the abbots of Orval and Elant.

Item 58: The complaint of the abbot of Eaunes against the abbess of Goujon, both in the diocese of Toulouse, was placed in the hands of the abbots of L'Escaledieu and Bonnefont, to whom also was committed the complaint of the abbot of Perigniac against that abbess.

Item 59: The complaint of the abbot of Villers-en-Brabant against the abbess of Salzinnes was placed in the hands of the abbots of les Dunes and Cambron.

---

[85] *The Acta of Hugh of Wells, Bishop of Lincoln, 1209–1235*, ed. David M. Smith, Lincoln Record Society 88 (Woodbridge, England, 2000), no. 447.

Item 60: The complaint of the abbess of Val-Saint-Tronde against the abbess of Hocht was placed in the hands of the abbots of Val-Saint-Lambert and Grandpré.

Item 61: The correction and reform of the abbey of nuns of Droitevaux was committed to the abbots of Acey and Bethune.

Item 62: Correction and reform of the nuns of Tarrant-Keynes in Dorset was placed in the hands of the abbots of Boxley in Kent and Robertsbridge in Sussex.

Item 63: Correction of the deviations of the nuns of Notre-Dame-de-l'Isle at Auxerre which have been judged to be contrary to the obedience to the norms of the Order was committed to the abbots of Fontmorigny in the diocese of Bourges and Mores in the diocese of Troyes.

Item 64: The prioress of Moncey has received multiple warnings from abbots and monks that she obey the Order. She has been wielding the pastoral staff when according to the principles of the Order she ought to be enclosed, has excluded abbot-visitors by force of arms, and has been acting rebelliously against the Order, and is therefore deposed. And the subprioress and portress who have supported her in this rebelliousness are also deposed by the authority of the General Chapter. The abbots of the house called Champagne in the diocese of le Mans and that of Clairmont should take care of this business. If the culprits are found to be unyielding, they should be punished as those abbots see fit. If it is necessary, the abbots should pronounce them excommunicate by the authority of the General Chapter. The prioress should be sent to another house and not allowed to return except by the authority of the General Chapter. The two abbots should reconcile and absolve those who are penitent.

Item 65: The abbess of Marquette, who has had her novices blessed by the archdeacon of Tournai against the norms and obedience to the Order, and who has also been stubborn and disobedient to the abbot-visitors of the Order which is contrary to the constitution of the Order, is punished by three days penance, one of them on bread and water, and exclusion for forty days from the choir stall of the abbess. The visitors from Clairvaux who look into this business are given full power, if they find her guilty, to punish her as she deserves.

Item 66: The abbess of Heiligenkreuz in Saxony, who refused to receive a visitor, and was therefore excommunicated from the divine service by him, is immediately deposed, sent to another house, and will be ineligible to be re-elected. . . .

Item 67: The abbess and nuns of Parc-Notre-Dame when they heard from their abbot visitors about the edicts adopted by the General Chapter last year, rose up together and said that they would never obey them or the Order on these issues. Clapping their hands together back and forth, they left the Chapter, threatening and striking their visitors. Then the abbot visitors waited until the ninth hour for the nuns to return to their Chapter in obedience to the Order; in the meantime, the nuns having driven them out had barred the gates against them. When this house was placed under interdict by those visitors for this obstinacy, and the widest sentence of excommunication issued against the rebels, the nuns solemnly sang Sext in full voices, asserting that the visitors, who should have been in charge, could not excommunicate their community of nuns, and that neither will they abstain from the divine office because of such a sentence, nor will they cede any power to them as visitors. The General Chapter declared the abbess immediately deposed and sent her and the cellerar from this place to other houses. Visitors from Clairvaux who were charged with taking care of this were given full power to correct what they found there to correct, etc. . . .

Item 68: The abbess of Lieu-Notre-Dame at Romorantin . . . who did not open the gates to her visitor the abbot of L'Aumône when he knocked three or four times, although it was known that she was present, and also hired a secular guard to keep the gates closed and to repel the visitors, and who in many other ways failed to uphold the constitution of the Order, was deposed immediately. The abbots of Varennes and Aubepierres were charged with seeing to this business, and if her insubordination continues they should pronounce her excommunicate by the authority of the General Chapter and send her to another house and punish all the other nuns who are guilty. But they should reconcile and absolve the penitent.[86]

---

[86] *Statuta capitulorum generalium ordinis cisterciensis ab anno 1116 ad annum 1786*, ed. J.-M. Canivez, 8 vols. (Louvain, 1933), vol. 2, year 1243.

Glossary

All Saints Day. November 1.

All Souls Day. November 2.

Allod, allodial land. Land-holding on which no one else is lord.

Alpine pastures. See *Transhumance.*

Amortissement. See *Mainmort.*

Anchoress. A female recluse who retires to a secluded place to practice religion; some anchoresses were walled in to rooms attached to churches. See also *Hermit.*

Arpent. Measure of land in France equal to about an acre.

Ascension, feast of. The Thursday following Rogation Sunday, the latter being the fifth Sunday after Easter.

Assumption of the Blessed Virgin Mary, feast of. August 15.

Bordaria. A holding of indeterminate size found adjoining a mansus or village, usually added on to its boundaries at some time of expansion; often, but not always, smaller than a normal family holding.

Bouvier. A traditional measure of land in France, called bouvier because it constitutes the amount of land that can be plowed in a day by a team of oxen. The bouviers of one region may not be those of another.

Brandon Sunday. First Sunday in Lent.

Candlemas. See *Purification of the Virgin, feast of the.*

Cartulary. A collection of charter copies put together by a religious corporation, family, or other group in the medieval period, most often by copying charters into a book or codex, occasionally onto a parchment roll. The motives of the cartulary maker might vary slightly from those who had written the original charters.

Cell, monastic cell. A small offshoot of a larger monastic community, sometimes a group sent out to colonize a new area, sometimes a group that is independently founded and attaches itself to an existing monastic community.

Cens. Traditional nominal annual payment from tenant to landowner in formal acknowledgment of ownership, usually paid in money rather than in kind. In contrast, the harvest rent—often called *terrage*—was in kind and often a percentage of the harvest. In cities, the original owner of the land might collect *cens*, while the developer who had put up buildings would collect rent.

Censive. Territory in which a particular person traditionally is owed *cens*. In the rural world there were often other owners to whom was paid a proportion of the harvest, and in cities there were owners who had constructed the buildings.

Chapter. The meeting of or the assembly of nuns of a community coming together at regular intervals, often daily, in a specific room of the monastery called the Chapter House.

Charter. A parchment record of a transaction between two individuals, one of them often ecclesiastical, most often recording the buying, selling, renting, mortgaging, exchange or arbitration of dispute over land or other rights to property. Written in Latin or the vernacular, often by a public or royal scribe who is sometimes described as working at the request of the parties to the transaction.

Common fields or *open fields*. Fields cultivated under a single regime of agriculture by an entire village without boundaries, but with individual villagers having marked strips within them.

Condomina. Literally a co-lordship, but could be used to describe a particular holding, similarly to saying "in that acreage."

Devotee. A person devoted to the religious practice but possibly not yet having taken formal vows.

Fief or *fevum*. A land holding granted by a superior, sometimes that granted by a lord to a vassal, but more often that granted by a lord to a tenant-cultivator.

General Chapter. The annual meeting of the heads of houses of a religious Order. The Cistercian General Chapter, thus, which met each year in September at Cîteaux was an annual universal assembly of all abbots of the Order with, at first, a parallel assembly of all abbesses. The latter was soon suppressed.

Grange. Literally a barn, but coming to mean the entire built-up farmstead, and in the usage of the twelfth-century monastic reformers, the entire farm often made up of consolidated holdings but located at some distance from the abbey center and therefore usually worked by hired laborers or lay-brothers and lay-sisters.

Hearth-tax. Annual tax on all households within a town or city.

Hermit. One who retires to a secluded place to practice religion alone or in a very small group, in contrast to living within a community of other religious men or women who share meals, mass, and religious office together.

Hof. A family farming unit, not so different from a mansus.

Honor. The administrative holding with its revenues of an official, for example, a countship or county.

Ides. In the ancient Roman calendar, the fifteenth day of March, May, July, and October, and the thirteenth day of the other months. Can count in descending order towards ides, as in nones and kalends.

Kalends. The first day of each month in the ancient Roman calendar. As with nones, one can count up to the kalends in descending order, so that the last day of the previous month is the second kalends, etc., all the way back to the previous ides. The fifth kalends of October would fall in September, etc.

Lateran Councils. Universal meetings of bishops and clergy at the Lateran Palace in Rome; of particular note is the Fourth Lateran held in 1215, which regularized many aspects of Christian practice.

Lay-sister/Lay-brother. A convert to the religious life in the new religious Orders of the High Middle Ages who was expected to perform only a truncated version of the divine office, and did not aim (because of humility, preference, or lack of intellectual training) to become a monk or nun of the choir. Eventually there is class identification, and knights cannot become lay-brothers or peasant women choir nuns.

Lent. The forty weekdays (including Saturdays) of Christian fasting (usually by abstaining from meat and other animal products) and penitence before Easter to commemorate Jesus' fasting in the wilderness.

Liege-man. A loyal follower or vassal; usually your liege-man holds directly from you.

Lord. A person having direct power over you; a ruler, master, or owner and head of a feudal estate.

Lordship. Having the power or authority of a lord, or the territory over which a lord holds power.

Mainmort. Religious corporations were considered to hold feudal land in mainmort, meaning that because that land was held not by a vassal but by a corporation that never died, such land could never pass back to the lord or king as a fief to be re-granted (for a tax called relief) to the next generation. Grants of such land to religious corporations were to be made only with a permission, called amortissement, from the superior lord or king, which gave the community rights to perpetual owner-ship. Amortissement was thus the giving away of the lord's re-granting privilege.

Manor. An estate or farm, usually but not always in one consol-idated location, belonging to an ecclesiastical or secular land-lord. Manors were cultivated by land-lords, using dependent peasants (or serfs) as laborers working either directly on the lord's lands or paying a percentage of the harvest on fields that they held from that lord.

Mansus. Originally meant a farmstead with lands sufficient to support a single peasant family, but by the High Middle Ages, because production got better, it appears that a half or quarter *mansus* might support a family.

Mills. Originally mills were the hand grinders or kerns for grind-ing, not unlike mortar and pestle, but in size and shape roughly like a rolling pin in a flat trough. In the ancient world these began to be replaced by donkey mills, in which animals pushed a wheel round and round on a flat surface on which grain was ground. Water-powered and wind-powered grinding mills were available in ancient times but were introduced widely through Europe only in the Middle Ages.

Monastic cell. See *cell.*

Mortgage. Not quite the same as what we think of today, the medieval mortgage was a contract by which land was trans-ferred to the lender as a pledge for a loan. Mortgages were extremely onerous because all the produce of the land went to the lender until the original owner repays.

Mountain pastures. See *Transhumance.*

Muid, measure, modium. Literally means measure. For dry ingredients a muid, although varying from one small region to the next, was roughly half a bushel in volume; in liquid perhaps double that.

Nones. In ancient Roman calendar the ninth day before the ides of the month, hence, the 7th of March, May, July, and October, and the 5th of other months. After the kalends, days up to the nones days are counted in descending order thus: the third nones, the second nones (the day before the nones), the nones. (Nones can also be the ninth hour of the liturgical day which is about nine hours after sunrise or about 3 PM).

Noval lands. Lands on which tithes had not previously been assessed.

Obol. A half penny.

Palm Sunday. Sixth Sunday in Lent, last before Easter.

Patronage. Support of religious communities by a variety of donors or patrons making gifts to those communities. Occasionally a particular individual or family is designated patron of a monastic community and granted specific rights such as burial in the monastic church.

Perche. A measure of land, probably less than an acre, but varying from region to region.

Purification of the Virgin, feast of the. February 2, also called *Candlemas.*

Saint Andrew, feast of. November 30.

Saint Hilary, feast of. January 13.

Saint John the Baptist, feast of nativity of. June 24.

Saint Martin, (winter) feast of. November 11.

Saint Michael, feast of. September 29.

Saint Peter, feast of the Chains of. August 1.

Saint Rémy, feast of. October 1.

Sauveté. Safeguarded village, usually newly founded.

Seal. The hardened wax marking a contract's authenticity, usually hanging from the parchment. It was made by impressing on softened wax (or for papal bulls on lead) a carefully-guarded royal, episcopal, personal or community seal matrix carrying a design that would reveal the sealer's identity. The seal matrix was usually made of metal, and seals were attached by silk threads, knitted twine, leather thongs, or by partially cutting away a strip from the edge of the parchment.

Sealing clause. Many of the charters included in this volume have clauses at the end telling the reader that the writer of the charter guarantees the contents or fortifies an agreement by making the impression of his seal.

Seigneur/seigneurialism. French for lord and lordship. See *Lord* and *Lordship.*

Sestier. Probably a sixth of a muid, something more than a quart, and a twelfth of the liquid muid.

Simony. The sin of buying and selling of Church office or the sacraments.

Squire. Young man of knightly class and training, not yet knighted, increasingly in thirteenth century may not ever be knighted because of expense.

Talent. A measure of weight varying from place to place, particularly used for precious metal.

Tallage. A head tax.

Tithes. Ecclesiastical revenue of one tenth of the produce of a field, etc.

Transhumance. Pastoralism practiced by seasonally moving animals from one elevation to another.

Villa. Can mean a manor or estate, but could also mean a village.

Visitor/visitation. Inspector for annual inspection of a religious house. Originally this was done by the bishop, but with exempt Orders like the Cistercians, visitation was practiced internally by father-abbots, often of neighboring houses.

Further Suggestions for Reading

Berman, Constance H. *Medieval Agriculture, the Southern-French Countryside, and the Early Cistercians. A Study of Forty-three Monasteries*. Philadelphia, Penn., 1986.

————. *The White Nuns: Women and Property Management in the Twelfth- and Thirteenth-Century Cistercian Order*. Forthcoming.

Burton, Janet. *The Yorkshire Nunneries in the Twelfth and Thirteenth Centuries*. Borthwick Paper 56. York, 1979.

Bynum, Caroline Walker. *Jesus as Mother: Studies in the Spirituality of the High Middle Ages*. Berkeley, Calif., 1982.

Elkins, Sharon. *Holy Women of Twelfth-Century England*. Chapel Hill, N.C., 1988.

Freed, John. "Urban Development and the 'Cura Monialium' in Thirteenth-century Germany," *Viator* 3 (1972), 311–27.

Gayoso, Andrea. "The Lady of Las Huelgas: A Royal Abbey and its Patronage," *Cîteaux* 51 (2000), 91–115.

Gilchrist, Roberta. *Gender and Material Culture: The Archaeology of Religious Women*. London, 1994.

Golding, Brian. *Gilbert of Sempringham and the Gilbertine Order c. 1130–c. 1300*. Oxford, 1995.

Hidden Springs: Cistercian Monastic Women: Medieval Religious Women 3:1. Ed. John A. Nichols and Lillian Thomas Shank. Kalamazoo, Mich., 1995.

Johnson, Penelope D. *Equal in Monastic Profession. Religious Women in Medieval France.* Chicago, 1991.

Jordan, Erin. "Prayer, Patronage, and Polders: Assessing Cistercian Foundations in Thirteenth-Century Flanders and Hainaut," *Cîteaux* (forthcoming).

Kerr, Berenice M. *Religious Life for Women circa 1100–circa 1350: Fontevraud in England.* Oxford, 1999.

Leyser, Henrietta. *Hermits and the New Monasticism. A Study of Religious Communities in Western Europe, 1000–1150.* London, 1984.

McNamara, Jo Ann Kay. *Sisters in Arms. Catholic Nuns through Two Millennia.* Cambridge, Mass., 1996.

Oliva, Marilyn. *The Convent and the Community in late Medieval England. Female Monasteries in the Diocese of Norwich 1350–1450.* Woodbridge, 1998.

Thompson, Sally. *Women Religious. The Founding of English Nunneries after the Norman Conquest.* Oxford, 1991.

Venarde, Bruce. *Women's Monasticism and Medieval Society: Nunneries in France and England, 890–1215.* Ithaca, N.Y., 1997.

Waldman, Thomas A. "Abbot Suger and the Nuns of Argenteuil," *Traditio* 41 (1985), 239–71.